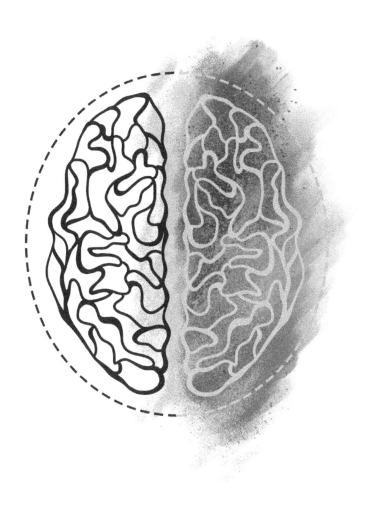

Pattern Breakers

Create healthy patterns, maintain boundaries, and cultivate empathy in the workplace and beyond.

Daniel Jacob Hill

Get free video trainings, resources, and much more by visiting

Mypatternbreaker.com

Acknowledgments

With deep gratitude I would like to dedicate this book to love, joy. The lessons you taught me gave me permission to explore myself, learn to play, and create better understanding of the relationship I hold with myself and with the world.

I would also like to thank the team that made this book possible.

To the best couch I could ever ask for, Lyn Christian, thank you for helping me turn my dream into a reality and for pushing me to go above and beyond.

For my editor, Jen Singleton, thank you for the organization and editing of this book. This wouldn't have been possible without you in my court.

To the talented artist, Ryan Rydalch. Thank you for creating such beautiful visuals and artwork for this book. The book cover turned out better than I imagined.

To my family, friends, and teachers. Thank you for always believing in me and supporting my work.

Table of Contents

Preface

Hello, and thank you for picking up this book. Before we get started, I'd like to introduce myself and give you some history to help explain why I decided to write this text.

My name is Daniel Jacob Hill. I was born and raised in Salt Lake City, Utah. I graduated from high school at the age of 16. No, I wasn't some child prodigy; I just knew how to work the public school system. And, unfortunately, like most teenagers, I thought I knew everything.

After I graduated from high school, I received an internship at my local LGBTQ resource center, The Utah Pride Center, and immediately enrolled at Salt Lake Community College (SLCC) where I studied social work. It seemed like the most logical place for a young, queer kid in Utah to land. I completed my six-month internship, and was offered a full-time position as the Youth Program Coordinator. I worked in the Utah Pride Youth Activity Center, which offered adolescents from the ages of 14 to 20 an after school drop-in center, a public kitchen, and activities such as art shows, youth drag shows, movie nights, game nights, and educational forums to involved them in volunteer opportunities and local politics.

This is where most people would say, "Ok, you're on a path toward something good." But a year into the job, I realized I wasn't cut out for social work. Feeling as though I needed a blank slate, I decided to quit my job and drop out of college.

I spent the summer bouncing from job to job, working as a barista for a brief time, then at a local clothing boutique as well as doing a bit of male modeling, all of which were unsuccessful and underwhelming.

Despite my seemingly aimless wandering, these experiences weren't for nothing. Modeling led me to a hair show where I was a hair model for a local cosmetology school called Taylor Andrews Academy of Hair Design. It was a wonderful experience—the energy, the creativity, the chaos—I had to be a part of it! A week later, I enrolled at Taylor Andrews.

I began cosmetology school in the summer of 2008 and graduated 11 months later. After graduation, I worked full-time at a salon called Star 21. I also landed a job as an educator with the international beauty product company UNITE, traveling around the country teaching product knowledge classes, styling courses, and presenting hair-cutting techniques. And in 2009, I was hired on as a contract worker at Utah Opera and Symphony as a wig and makeup artist. It was a lot of hard work. But by the age of 20, I felt like I had managed to engineer the perfect career.

But by 2013, my enthusiasm started to shift. I felt anxious, uncertain; I felt I was missing something. I moved to San Diego to work full-time for UNITE in their education department and at the UNITE Salon. This lasted less than a year.

While I was there, I said yes to everything. When they wanted to pull me out of the salon, I said yes. When they asked me to work full-time in the corporate offices, I said yes. When I was asked to stay late, work weekends, travel two hours a day to get to work, I said yes. I ignored what I wanted or needed. And I never stood up for myself. I felt frustrated and overwhelmed. I felt like a water balloon waiting for the inevitable smack. I thought it was because I couldn't handle the job. But really, I didn't understand how to handle myself.

In 2014, I moved back to Salt Lake City and picked up where I left off. I went back to Star 21, went back to Utah Opera, and still did the occasional teaching jobs with UNITE (I didn't completely burn that bridge). I decided to re-enroll at SLCC and finish my degree, which had been on hold for eight years.

"This time," I thought, "I'm going to get it right." I switched my major to Psychology. I also switched salons. The owner, Nick, and I instantly clicked. It seemed like overnight we became best friends. We shared everything—our goals, our fears, our history, our passions. He also offered a wealth of knowledge about hairdressing.

My career was going really well. And in January 2016, something amazing happened—I fell in love. It was unexpected and amazing. I met Kevin while working on a production of *The Merry Widow* at Utah Opera. I thought he was the most handsome, charming, funny man I'd ever met.

It seemed like I had it all—a fantastic job, an amazing boyfriend, a beautiful condo—but again something didn't feel right. By late summer, Nick was pressuring me to become his business partner; I wasn't ready. I told him, "If you need a business partner now, and can't wait until I'm done with school, then I'm not sure I'm the right person." A week later, Nick decided to close the salon permanently and our friendship began to fall apart.

I was able to find a chair to rent at another salon. However, I missed Nick and his salon, I missed my old co-workers, and my old work life. I was miserable and losing focus.

By the end of 2016 I had graduated college and was feeling more comfortable at my new salon. I even secured a temporary wig and makeup position at Utah Opera where I designed the hair and makeup for the production of *La Bohème* and *The Long Walk*, and co-designed for Don Giovanni. I thought things were looking up.

But in July of 2017, Kevin ended our relationship. He said he loved me but could no longer be with me. It didn't make sense. What confidence I'd regained vanished. I began drinking heavily. I gained weight. I didn't care about my work anymore. I would go into the salon and cry; I would drive in the car and cry; I would look at clothes Kevin bought me and cry. I was a mess. My world was falling apart. How could I loose my best friend, the love of my life, and the best job I'd ever had in one year? I was lonely, anxious and depressed.

Eventually, despite how miserable I felt, it was time to take a good, hard look at myself. Something was getting in the way of my career and my relationships.

Why do I share all this with you? It's simple. My past, my journey, the experiences I hold, the gritty details I have left out for the moment highlight a painful truth—I was never taught how to cultivate emotional wellbeing. In fact, most people could probably say the same, especially those of us in the service industry. We're never taught strategies to reduce negative emotions or harmful self-talk. We're never taught how to manage stress, how to be assertive and express difficult emotions when necessary, how to stay proactive instead of reactive, or how to bounce back after adversity.

With help, I realized that in my determined race toward a prosperous career, I was overlooking a key element of success—my emotional needs. I was letting destructive behavioral patterns dictate the outcomes in my life. After years of sabotaging my own artistic energies, I realized I needed new patterns and habits if I wanted different results. I needed a system of self-care.

With much trial and error, I began eliminating the things that hindered my success—smoking and drinking. And I began introducing practices that supported my success—reading self-care books, finding a therapist, and practicing yoga regularly. Slowly, as I changed my daily patterns, I realized I was creating a structure that could support what I was actually craving—more creative flow, more passion and more awareness.

This is what inspired me to create this book. I had to learn these lessons the hard way—from my mistakes. But my hope is to share the strategies I've learned for creating a system of self-care with others like me. While making mistakes is all good and fine when you add in a little hindsight and self-compassion, it's also nice to have some help along the way too.

For those of you who continue reading, I encourage you to keep an open mind and an open heart.

—Daniel Jacob Hill

Introduction

To devote one's self to this craft, there is a price to be paid, it seems. As hair-care and beauty professionals, we spend much of our time caring for other people's needs. In the process, our own needs sometimes get lost, forgotten or shoved to the far reaches of our awareness because there is just not enough time or energy left in a day to manage them. I know many stylists who drink heavily, smoke a pack of cigarettes a day, use drugs regularly, and find other unhealthy ways to "unwind" after seeing 10 to 20 clients a day. (I should know. I was that person.) We cripple ourselves with habitual patterns and coping mechanisms that hinder our potential.

Over the past ten years while traveling the globe as an educator, I've met a vast number of hairdressers from the United States, Europe and Australia. They all have a few things in common. They all have the knowledge it takes to run their businesses. They all have the technical cutting, coloring, and styling skills to be successful hairdressers. And they all share a passion for what they do. And yet, the majority seem to lack one crucial instrument—self-care. The hair industry is replete with blogs, websites, videos, books, and hands-on technical and educational courses on how to grow your business or sharpen your skills. But there isn't a whole lot out there for people in the service industry on how to attend to one's emotional wellbeing, a key aspect of any career.

This book is intended to offer people, like me, a way to manage life and a career in the hair industry. It's a guidebook on how to understand our clients and ourselves better. This book is written directly to cosmetologists.

Although, the same principles can be applied to all people within the service industry—tattoo artists, estheticians, massage therapists, nail technicians, bartenders, dentists, doctors, nurses, the list is endless. If you're a person who provides a service, and works one-on-one with individuals in a close environment, this book is written for you. It will assist you in creating healthy patterns and maintaining boundaries in the workplace and beyond. This book is sectioned out to help you understand yourself before you try to understand your clients. It is not to be powered through in an afternoon. You'll want to reference back as you practice the concepts expressed. It is a workbook that you'll want to revisit many times over.

I invite you to begin a journey of self-exploration. I offer techniques for building a stable foundation of self-care. It begins with recognizing and understanding your patterns, establishing healthy boundaries, and cultivating a practice of empathy. As you build upon this foundation, you will find opportunities to achieve, acquire and cultivate what you desire in life and in your career.

This is a workbook filled with many writing exercises. I highly recommend you get a journal or notebook to follow along. This will help you see your progression from beginning to end. Don't worry too much about how it's constructed, use what is comfortable and accessible. Don't skip the writing exercises, you'll miss out on the important insights held here. By committing to the exercises, you will better understand how to perform and operate at your full potential. Take each chapter at your own pace, do the exercises, re-read the chapter, and really understand the content before moving on to the next chapter. This is a workbook, so do the work.

Pattern Breakers

Chapter 1 Fear

The voice of change

"Fear is excitement without the breath."

—Fritz Perls

Whenever I try something new, there is often a loathsome little voice niggling inside my head—"What are you doing? This is stupid. No one wants this." On more than one occasion, it has nearly crushed my enthusiasm for a challenge. (And believe me, that obnoxious voice is doing its best right now.) But I've learned that whenever my fussy friend starts shouting criticisms, I know I'm on the right track. I know I'm about to attempt something bold, wiggle into new territory, or experiment with a new idea. I know I am just experiencing fear as the first step to change.

Why is fear the wet blanket of change? To put it succinctly, it's because the outcome is always uncertain. And as humans, we detest uncertainty. Change always elicits fear— the fear of failure, the fear of rejection, the fear of discovering unpleasant truths—it's all fear of the unknown. You can expect fear to arise in a variety of different life experiences—graduating from college, beginning a new job, moving out of state, going on a first date, telling someone you love them for the first time, anything that is new or pushes the boundaries of your comfort zone.

Story Time!

When I relocated to San Diego to work for UNITE, I never imagined I'd come back to Utah. I was moving to the best beach city on earth to work for a company and a brand I believed in. It seemed like a dream job.

But after a few months, I was pulled away from the salon to work exclusively in the office. I tried to rationalize the shift— Even thought I didn't have access to the creativity and energy of a salon, I was still working for an amazing company in an amazing city. What did I have to lose, right?

But after suffering behind a desk for months, I found myself feeling overwhelmed and miserable. It was like trying to push a very exuberant elephant into a keyhole. I had to make a choice—stay in a job I hated or deal with my fear of failure and move back to Utah. What would people think of me? I'd moved away to attain a dream and it shattered in my hands.

Eventually, I tucked the fear, the feelings of inadequacy and the nasty self-talk into my back pocket and moved back to my old life in Utah. At first, all I felt was shame. Until I picked my head up and looked at what I had really gained from the experience—I was a better hairdresser, a better business person, and had I more confidence with things I never expected to be good at. If I hadn't pushed through my fear of failure and made the hard choice to reboot, I would never have found this inner wisdom.

I share pieces of my life and other people's stories too because, when I was trying to make some difficult changes and deal with uncertainty, I wish I had read stories like these. When I was lost, wandering and aching, I wish someone had told me that we all feel fear, even successful, smart, funny, strong people.

As you work through the process of building your own system of self-care, the voice of doubt will inevitably begin whispering fearful grumblings. Fortunately, you (as a successful, smart, funny, strong person) are well on your way to acknowledging these fears. Remember: fear is the emotion that can either stop you from reaching your goals, or it can push you to new limits and new possibilities.

8 Actions—Standing Up to Fear

We all want to create amazing lives—we all want to feel better, generate more success, become more self-aware, or make more money. Unfortunately, when it's time to take responsibility for manifesting our desires, fear can weaken our resolve. It's a lot easier to dream about a better life than to fail trying to obtain it.

This is why I have identified eight actions that are necessary if you want to begin standing up to your fears and begin cultivating the life you want.

Taking aim: The first step in standing up to your fear is deciding you are going to change. This includes acknowledging where you are and setting sights on where you want to be. Then you make the commitment to find the path between these two points.

Showing up: The hardest part of making changes to your life is often just showing up. For example, I hear people say that the hardest part of their day is waking up and getting out of bed. But once they've taken that first step, the rest of the day flows naturally. People also say that getting to the gym is the hardest part of their workout. But once they get to the gym, the workout is great. Sometimes all you need to push past your fear is to take one small step toward your goal.

Cultivating choices: Albert Einstein is widely credited with saying, "The definition of insanity is doing the same thing over and over again, but expecting different results." In order to make changes to your life, you have to start with making new choices, which means you need to try new things. Some of the choices will help you toward your goal and other choices won't. The key here is to be open about what works and what doesn't.

Accepting imperfection: When you try new things, don't expect to do them perfectly. Nobody is perfect. The first draft of any writing project, painting, or musical score is always flawed. Your life changes are no exception. You'll get there if you accept that you have to edit your work.

Letting go: There are things in this life that we can control and those that we can't. It's important to stop and think: "Is this something I can control?" If it is beyond your control (like how others are behaving), let it go!

Finding strategies: This action is about understanding what works for you. If you need more clarity on how to proceed, what strategies help you with self-awareness? Taking a walk, talking to a friend, writing in a journal, drawing a picture, exercise—whatever it may be, it's important to find your personal strategies that help when you feel stuck. Remember, this can and should include things that are outside your comfort zone.

Owning failure: Not every attempt at change will be successful. Owning the fact that you will sometimes fail can be liberating. Once you realize that failure isn't a stopping point and only a chance to learn something, you'll be ready to take on the next challenge.

Embracing the unexpected: Just because you've charted a coarse toward a particular goal doesn't mean that when you arrive, it will look like what you expected. Any career, life path or relationship can take an unexpected turn. Don't get fixated on the destination. Step back and notice the journey too. You're bound to find wisdom in unexpected places. As one of my yoga teachers, Becka Cooper, says, "It's not about the destination, the journey is the destination."

By taking these actions, you will begin to shift and evolve. And those fears you feel will become guideposts as you begin operating at your full potential. In this book, I reference operating at your full potential a lot. What I mean by this is that you will begin to see how shifting perspective and patterns can allow you to view yourself and the world around you differently. You will begin to achieve goals that you may have struggled with in the past, you will begin to cultivate healthy relationships around you, and elevate your personal and professional life, grow your business, and attract new people and opportunities.

In order to elevate your life and operate at your full potential you'll need to explore your existing patterns and break the ones that hinder your progress. I've designed a series of writing exercise to help you begin examining your patterns. These exercises will help you to see where you are now and where you want to go. They will help you design your life and follow the path you desire.

Writing Exercise: What are Your Fears?

This first writing exercise is designed to help you begin exploring your fears. By committing pen to paper, you can activate parts of your brain and access different realms of self-awareness. Don't get hung up on what your journal should look like. Make it easy. The key here is to gain new perspectives.

In a quiet space without distraction, begin first by taking 10 minutes to just think. Think about one thing you desire. This can be anything—a new job, a better relationship with someone, a healthier body. As you think about what you desire, notice the voice of fear. Notice the negative grumblings of your inner critic.

The next step is to begin writing. Write down the fears that may be holding your desire captive. Write what scares you, making sure to note why you think you are afraid. As you write about your fears (in whatever format you prefer), examine how the 8 Actions of standing up to fear can help you see a potential path through your fear toward your desires. For example, I was scared to write this book, to share it with the public. I had to be open and vulnerable and explore my fear of rejection and failure. It was the first step (and the only way I could see) in accomplishing something I wanted. By bringing fear to the front of your mind, you'll begin to cultivate a practice of honesty and vulnerability with yourself. This is an important first step as you move toward what you want.

Analyzing fears and emotions can be difficult. Not only is it difficult to take action to fight fears, sometimes we may not even know what they are. Throughout this book I use writing as my guide to understand myself better. However, I recognize that not all people can sit and write. There are plenty of other paths toward clarity.

Story Time!

My friend, Jude, is a stunningly talented drag performer. They perform as a drag queen and drag king—meaning they do not identify as one gender. Jude sometimes expresses their drag performances as masculine or feminine depending on what the performance demands. Jude illuminates their emotions, feelings, and fears and explores them through performance art. Each one of their numbers is a story of self-exploration and self-expression. This talented individual slays the stage and gives a powerful, heart-felt performance that is raw and unapologetic. It allows Jude the space to quiet their fears, anxieties, and frustrations.

If writing is not your cup of tea, explore other ways of examining your fears. This could be through art—things like painting, drawing, sculpting or performing. Perhaps it's something as simple as taking a hike, being in nature, or going on a bike ride. Find something that creates clarity and peace of mind, something that allows space and opportunity for your mind to explore emotions and fears. Don't doubt your process. Doubt is just the precursor to fear.

By recognizing your fears, you can begin to move past them and work with them. If fear becomes present at any time, take a breath. Like the quote at the beginning of this chapter says, "Fear is nothing but excitement without the breath." Take a nice big exhale and allow a new breath to fill your body and unleash the excitement.

RECAP:

Change always elicits fear.

Remember that fear is the emotion that can either stop you from reaching your goals, or it can drive you toward new limits and new possibilities.

Practice the 8 Actions in Standing up to Fear.

Chapter 2 Patterns

What are patterns?

"We know what we are but not what we may be."
—Ophelia in William Shakespeare's Hamlet

Patterns are seen everywhere: the lunar cycles, the seasonal shifts, the cycle of life. You could say the entire universe is a system of patterns. All patterns serve a purpose and hold significant meaning.

Patterns also exist on a much smaller, personal level. These are patterns of behavior, routines or habits that dictate our lives. Some may be obvious, while others reside just under the surface of our awareness. Most of our daily activities follow specific patterns: the time we wake up or go to bed, when and what we eat, how we hold our bodies, even the route we take to and from work. Most of these routine behaviors and habits are beneficial. They free the brain from making an infinite number of decisions all day long so it can engage in more important and creative thinking. Patterns are tools that allow us to navigate the world.

Patterns can establish moments of ease and flow, but they can also restrict our creativity, efficacy and success. Patterns solve problems and create problems. With a little help, we can see these patterns for what they really are. By taking the time to understanding our patterns, we can keep what elevates us and disassemble what hinders us, gradually shifting toward growth, understanding and our full potential. To do this, we begin by focusing on three distinct kinds of patterns—behavioral patterns, relationship patterns and daily patterns.

The 3 Patterns

Behavioral Patterns: Behavioral patterns are reoccurring actions (habits) an individual takes toward a given situation or object. Two examples might be the steps you take to alleviate feelings of anxiety or stress after a hard day at work, or the process you go through to safely drive home at night. Each of these examples would incorporate personal habits. In the first example, you might make a habit of having a glass of wine or taking a hot bath after work. In the second, you might always check your mirrors before turning on the ignition, or always look over your shoulder before changing lanes.

Patterns of behavior are often quite complex and need a certain amount of self-awareness to understand. For example, if a person wants to lose weight, they have to change their eating and exercise habits. But sometimes this same person may engage in emotional eating and put off exercise because they believe it will take too much time. (I speak from experience. I love nothing more than a pint of ice cream, French fries, and a rom com movie when I feel sad and emotional.) A path to weight loss means this individual must address the individual habits of emotional eating and procrastination as well as the underlying reasons for these habits.

Relationship Patterns: Next, we have relationship patterns. These are patterns we maintain with clients, friends, lovers or family members. Our relationship patterns dictate the kind of people we develop relationships with, how we interact with certain people, and how we let other people treat us. An example of a relationship pattern might be feeling like you need to always take care of your friends— help them get a good job, pick the right partner or design a wardrobe. You might habitually choose friends who constantly need things. You may even see yourself as having the answers to all their problems. Over time, this becomes exhausting, one-sided and unsustainable. Learning to cultivate healthy boundaries will help you find and maintain healthy relationships.

Daily Patterns: Daily patterns are the foundation for how we function and interact in our day-to-day lives. These patterns add structure and give us a sense of certainty. An example might be having a predictable 9-to-5-work schedule. Many people rely on a daily pattern like this for reasons of personal security; they know when they work, how much money they can expect, and how to plan out other aspect of their lives like social activities. Daily patterns also include what time we wake up, when we go to bed, where we like to shop, and places we like to eat at.

Story Time!

I had a gentleman that came into the salon every three weeks for a haircut. I'd been cutting his hair for a year. In that year, he never wanted a different haircut. I developed a pattern of eliminating the consultation at the beginning of his appointments. I thought I already knew what he liked, and gave it to him every time. Why should I waste time doing a consultation every appointment? I realized this wasn't serving me in a professional manner. He may be getting the same haircut every appointment, but it is still my responsibility as a hairdresser to check in and see how he enjoyed his last haircut and perhaps give him new suggestions. I wasn't fulfilling my potential to be a better professional and I wasn't giving him an opportunity to voice his opinion. I committed to giving him and all my clients a consultation regardless of how many times I've seen them. With this particular gentleman he hasn't been interested in changing his haircut. I have had other clients who were

---

looking to change their style and the consultation allowed
them to express their idea of change.

This chapter outlines a process by which you can begin to illuminate your patterns and eventually shift them to your benefit. As you begin addressing your behavioral patterns, relationship patterns and daily patterns, it's helpful to remind yourself that your patterns are not dualistic—they are not black or white, good or bad. For example, stating that drinking is a bad pattern does nothing to address the underlying issue. Drinking is bad for your health, but it may help with stress and anxiety. With this information, how could you take the component of stress relief and create a new habit or pattern that solves the problem of anxiety?

Patterns are too complex to classify as good or bad, right or wrong. It's more important to analyze your patterns from the perspective of: are they hindering your potential or elevating your successes? Once you can answer this question then you can begin the work of creating new patterns to attain your desired results.

Writing Exercise: Pattern Recognition

The first step in attaining what you desire is to understand what elevates your success and what hinders your success. This means you must be able to reflect upon your own behavioral, relationship and daily patterns. Bringing awareness to your patterns is a powerful tool toward shifting the outcome of your life.

There are three stages to bringing awareness: Think, Say and Act. This writing exercise is designed to help you bring awareness to your patterns and eventually take steps in creating change.

Think: In a quiet space without distraction, take 10 minutes to just think. Think about one thing you desire. This can be anything—a new job, a better relationship with someone, a healthier body. As you contemplate what you desire, begin formulating ideas about what patterns might be elevating your ability to be successful and what patterns might be hindering your success. Notice if these are behavioral patterns, daily patterns or relationship patterns.

Say: In your journal, state one clear, concise desire. Then create two columns. Label the first column Elevate, and label the second column Hinder. Under the Elevate column, list patterns in your life that you feel are helpful in achieving your desire. Under the Hinder column, list patterns in your life that you feel need improvement or hinder your success in achieving your desire. Here is an example of one of my Elevate/Hinder Lists.

I want to feel less stress at work.	
Elevate	**Hinder**
Working five days a week. Having a daily yoga practice. Balancing work and play. Staying sober. Seeing my family and friends. Keeping the house clean. Continuing my education. Taking time for myself.	Lacking enough sleep. (1)(D) Neglecting to take vacations. (5)(B) Neglecting to visit family regularly. (2)(R) Watching too much TV. (4)(R) Taking on too much at one time. (3)(B) Not spending enough time in nature. (7)(D)

Your lists don't need to be a long, just try to be honest with yourself. And notice if a particular item might need further exploration. The more time you spend creating your list, the better understanding you will gain. You will most likely start off with surface-level thoughts and emotions. By taking time to process your patterns before moving on, it's more likely you will be able to see, and set, a clear path to your desired outcome. Trust that you might find something unexpected or surprising.

Feel proud and grateful for the things that elevate you; you are already creating success. You should also feel good about identifying those patterns that might be hindering your progress; you are building your own road map. These patterns simply need to be reworked to help you achieve your desired goal.

Act: Begin by categorizing your Hinder list. Notice the numbers next to my Hinder patterns. These are ranked 1 (for most important) to 7 (least important)—seeing my family regularly is more important than taking a vacation. Rank your Hinder list items according to how important or necessary each item is to attaining your desire. For example, I feel it is most important that I get good sleep in order to feel less stress at work the next day. Having a level of importance will help you keep in mind what holds high and low priority as you take steps toward your desired goal.

Next, reflect upon the patterns in your life that might be draining precious energy. Ask yourself what type of pattern each Hinder list item might be—Behavioral Pattern, Daily Pattern, or Relationship Pattern. Mark each Hinder list item with a B, D or R to indicate the category. This will help you explore options for potential action you can take toward changing certain habits.

As you begin addressing your hindering patterns, it is important to work at them one at a time, at a comfortable pace. Starting with the Hinder list item you ranked as number 1, begin to explore ideas and strategies that could shift this hindering pattern into something that elevates you.

On paper, with words or pictures, explain the habits that constitute your highest ranked Hinder list item. For example, my highest ranked item (Lacking enough sleep) is a Daily Pattern. Each night, I maintained a habit of watching TV or scrolling through social media before I went to sleep. After researching how to sleep better, I realized the light from the screens was making it difficult for my brain to get the proper sleep signals. I was staying awake too long, not getting enough sleep hours at night. And I wasn't getting the quality, deep sleep I needed to feel rested in the morning. I was tired and distracted. Thus, I wasn't able to manage stress during the day very effectively.

The next step is seeing and designing a path from where you are (your current habits) to where you want to be (elevating habits). By breaking down your Hinder list items into specific habits, you can now pinpoint the habits that can be reshaped or changed. You will begin to notice subtle actions that you could take to design a better pattern. Going back to my example, I decided to take a few small actions that would shift my pattern of not getting enough sleep. I moved my electronics to a different room and made sure my sleeping area was dark and quiet. If I felt like watching TV or scrolling through social media at night, I would enjoy those activities in another room until I needed to go to bed. This helped my brain get the appropriate sleep signals at the appropriate time, and I began sleeping better at night.

I am not suggesting that every item on your list will be easy to reshape or change. But by understanding what hinders you, you can begin to make small steps toward your goal. Remember, some actions will be easy, others will be difficult, and some you may need help with. And it will take personal accountability as well as a desire to change. Fight your fearful inner critic and keep trying new ways to reshape and change patterns that making it hard for you to progress. (See Appendix References and Appendix Resources.)

Story Time!

When I decided to give up alcohol because it was interfering with all aspects of my life—my career, my relationship with friends, family and clients, and my self-esteem. I knew I needed help. I decided to see a therapist who suggested I start with a 30-day cleanse. She recommended the book, The 30-Day Sobriety Solution to help me along the way. After the 30-day cleanse, I felt great! I lost 10 pounds that month just by cutting out alcohol. This felt like a good start, but I needed more to help me from slipping back. She helped me recognize my triggers, get to the core of my drinking, and analyze why I was drinking. With her help and the help of friends and family, the journey toward sobriety became easier and easier. But it took time, patience, commitment, and motivation. And It definitely did not change overnight.

If this process feels overwhelming, don't worry. In Chapter 4, we will explore ways to create healthy daily patterns that help create an environment for success. For now, just Think, Say, and Act on one Hinder list item at a time, keeping in mind that you are making progress toward your desire.

This process is a powerful tool you can use whenever you need to gain more clarity and awareness for what you desire in life. It is an exercise that you will revisit many times as you progress through this workbook.

Visual Reminders

Having visual reminders is incredibly helpful as you work through your Hinder list. Make a copy of your Hider list and put it in an area where you see it frequently. As you address each item individually, write out a Commitment phrase for each item and post it next to the list. Begin by stating, *I commit to...* then explain how you intend to reshape what hinders you.

Read it out loud every time you pass by the list. My Hinder list and Commitment phrases are taped to my bathroom mirror. My Commitment phrases read:

I commit to . . .

Get more rest every night and create a daily habit of healthy sleep

See my parents on Sundays,

Meditate daily,

Fill my time with more fulfilling activities,

Plan more vacations for myself,

Work on gaining upper body strength so I can have more endurance at work, and

Enjoy at least 10 minutes every day outside.

Notice how I avoid negative words like "*don't*", "*not*", and "*no*". State your Commitment phrases as if they are already a success. Say, *I commit to a healthy sleep pattern*, rather than, *I commit to not staying up late.* Keep it positive and uplifting. Words are powerful.

Create accountability and actionability in your phrasing. Instead of saying, *I commit to seeing my parents more*, I phrase it as, *I commit to see my parents on Sundays.* This means I have a specific action I must take at a specific time. Thus, creating more clarity and accountability.

Breaking Old Habits

During this process, you may find that old habits or patterns resurface. That's okay! Do not beat yourself up if you fall back into old routines. Just acknowledge that you've fallen into an old pattern and resolve to try again. Creating these shifts in your life is a lot of work and can be challenging at times. Just remember, you are working toward something you desire and failures are just part of the journey.

RECAP:

Behavioral, relationship and daily patterns dictate the outcomes and successes in our lives.

Pattern recognition is the foundation to understand how and why we act and react in the world.

Focus on a single desire, then Think, Say and Act.

Create your Elevate/Hinder list to establish and recognize existing patterns and habits. Rate your patterns and habits, gradually work through one item at a time.

Turn your weaknesses into strengths by reworking your hindering patterns into patterns that elevates you.

Create visual reminders that you can revisit and read daily.

If you fall into old habits, that's okay! Pick up and try again. A flower doesn't blossom overnight. It takes time, patience, and nurturing.

Chapter 3 Boundaries

Creating and maintaining boundaries

"The greatest discovery of my generation is that human beings can alter their lives by altering their attitudes of mind." —William James

There are times in life when we find ourselves at a crossroads—we have the option to choose a path that supports what we desire or we can choose to put other people's needs and desires before our own. Those of us in the service industry are intimately acquainted with this choice: Do I say *yes* to a request from a client or risk losing their patronage by saying *no* sometimes? Unfortunately, you can't make the right choice, pick the right path without creating and maintaining boundaries.

So, what are boundaries? Let's define boundaries as your limits, a line in the sand you draw and will not cross. Boundaries hold space for your desires, values, self-esteem and potential growth. They define you and your actions.

Why are boundaries important? Maintaining consistent boundaries allows you the freedom to understand and explore your creativity, autonomy and self-efficacy. There are 3 essential steps to creating and maintaining boundaries:

Understand what you want.

Know your patterns.

Outline your path.

Understand what you want. Defining and maintaining boundaries isn't always easy. First, you have to have a clearly defined desire, a goal, in order to create and maintain a boundary. This is where the work you did in the previous chapter comes in handy. The first step in understanding your patterns was to verbalize something you desire. For example, my previously stated goal was to feel less stress at work. As you work toward creating and maintaining your boundaries, utilize the work you've accomplished in the previous chapter. Zero in on what you want and keep it front of mind.

Know your patterns. If you analyze your patterns, you can define your boundaries. I verbalized my desire to feel less stress at work so I could understand which patterns might be helping me achieve my goal and which patterns were hindering my success. As you begin shifting patterns that hinder your progress toward your desired goal, you will quickly realize you need to set some boundaries. In order to make change, you have to hold yourself accountable. For example, if I want to get more sleep so I don't feel stressed at work the next day, I have to get to bed at a reasonable hour. This might mean I have to leave a party early or decline a request by a client to work late. Use your pattern recognition exercise to help identify areas that need boundaries.

Outline your path. In order to get somewhere, you have to plan your route. By using the writing tool in the previous chapter to categorize your patterns in an Elevate/Hinder lists, you can see how setting boundaries makes it easier to make improvements to your day-to-day routines. You will use a similar technique in this next section to develop a plan for creating boundaries. Because the workplace can be unpredictable, one of the best places to start creating and maintain boundaries (especially for those of us within the service industry) is at work.

Define Your Job and Do It!

Before we get into too much detail on how to create boundaries at work, you need to first understand what your job is. Let me explain—I am a cosmetologist. I have a license in cosmetology. You can call me a hairdresser, stylist, beautician, whatever, but I am trained and certified as a cosmetologist. The Merriam-Webster dictionary defines a cosmetologist as: *a person licensed to provide cosmetic treatments to the hair, skin, and nails: one trained in cosmetology.* Nowhere in this definition does it say that I am a counselor, therapist, psychologist, food provider, valet, or any other roles I might be asked to play by a client. My job is to provide knowledge and cosmetic services to the hair, skin, and nails, nothing more and nothing less.

When I tell people I'm a hairstylist and that I'm interested in psychology, they invariably say things like, "You're a hairdresser. You're practically a therapist, listening to people's problems all day." No, I am not. I do not pretend to, nor do I try to provide a service that I am not remotely qualified to give.

Story Time!

When I first began a career in cosmetology, I would listen to everyone's problems, dramas, troubles, worries, and stories. I'd come home exhausted. After taking on everyone else's baggage, I could hardly handle my own. Hence, I used smoking, drinking, and drugs to find release and escape. I didn't hold boundaries and the price was my wellbeing.

Not maintaining boundaries can also affect your efficacy at work. I once worked with a woman who became very

---

enamored with energy work. She was so passionate about it that she began to do energy work on her clients when they came in for a hair appointment. She would dominate all conversation with her energy work experiences. Slowly, she became less and less busy. Her clients started going to other stylists. I'd hazard a guess that they left because she was performing energy work and not the job they were paying for.

The point is—do the job you were trained to do. The first step in establishing boundaries is to define your job. By understanding what your job is, by defining it, you have a clear map of where your boundaries should sit. By defining your job, you are setting a boundary for yourself and protecting yourself from falling into patterns that don't elevate you or your career.

When defining your job, you may use a literal textbook definition or perhaps your own definition, but write it down! You'll want to refer to this definition when you are feeling uncertain about choices you are forced to make at work. Once you have defined what your job is, you can begin to dig a little deeper, finding areas where you can create personal boundaries with your clients, friends and family to protect your integrity, take care of your wellbeing, and capitalize on your strengths.

Yes and No Test

The second step to cultivating boundaries is to recognize the areas in your personal and professional life that create feelings of happiness, success, and flow as well as patterns that create roadblocks, frustration, stress, and unease. I like to think of this exercise as your Yes and No list. It's as simple as it sounds, creating your boundaries around what is a "yes" for you and what is a "no." For example, a "no" for me is drinking alcohol or risking the integrity of someone's hair for the sake of a fad. An example of a "yes" would be: Yes, I accept new clients. Yes, I will commit to a daily yoga practice.

Writing Exercise: Flow and Block

We begin this writing exercise by revisiting the three stages of bringing awareness: Think, Say and Act.

Think: In a quiet space without distraction, take 10 minutes to just think. Think about your job/career and how you define it. In addition, contemplate what brings you feelings of happiness, success and flow in your personal life. Begin formulating ideas about what patterns might be elevating your ability to feel happiness, success and flow and what patterns create roadblocks, frustration, stress, and unease. Notice if these are behavioral patterns, daily patterns or relationship patterns.

Say: In your journal, create a two-column list—one side for FLOW, the other side for BLOCK. Under FLOW write down all the areas in your personal life that put you in a state of flow, happiness, or wellbeing. Under BLOCK write down all the things that seem to create roadblocks, frustration, or stress. Take as much time as you need to create this list. Below is an example of my FLOW & BLOCK list.

FLOW	BLOCK
Having a daily yoga practice.	Drinking alcohol.
Eating a vegetarian diet.	Staying out late.
Getting eight hours of sleep.	Binge watching TV.
Working no more than 6 days a week.	Worrying about finances and paying quarterly taxes.
Practicing mediation.	Not taking personal time for myself.
Spending time with friends	Saying yes to everything.

and family. Being completely booked solid at the salon. Continuing my own education. Cooking. Riding my bike. Writing and reading daily.	Letting other people's behavior affect me.

Once you have articulated FLOW & BLOCK in your personal life, think about things that create FLOW & BLOCK at work. In your journal, create another two-column list—one side for FLOW (clients and services that create flow), the other side for BLOCK (things that cause stress and/or need improvement). Here is one of my lists:

FLOW: Clients and services that create flow.	BLOCK: Things that cause stress and/or need improvement.
Natural highlights. Fashion colors and creative colors. Gray coverage, root touch ups. Up styles. Straight to mildly curly hair. Women's short hair (short layers and bobs). Adult clients between the ages of 20-70. Working with other artists. The ability to create my own schedule and manage my own retail.	Comprising the health of someone's hair. Chunky highlights. Military cuts. Extremely curly or coily hair. Children below the age of 5. Clients who ask for discounts. Being a sounding board for clients. Gaps in my salon schedule.

Act: Now that you have a list of items in your personal and professional life that facilitate happiness or satisfaction (FLOW) and a list of items that infuse frustration or stress (BLOCK), it's time to set your boundaries. Begin by writing Yes and No statements for your FLOW and BLOCK items. Feel free to group similar items together. Here's an example:

Yes, I will continue to incorporate daily habits like eating well, exercising, and connecting with friends and family to bring happiness and satisfaction into my life.

No, I will not compromise the health of someone's hair or discount my services.

Story Time!

A few years ago, I had a new client come into the salon wanting to go blonde for her friend's wedding. Her friend was getting married the next day. The client had fire engine red hair. We sat down and discussed in length what color of blonde she wanted, talked about her hair color history, how she styles her hair, and what products she uses. After a long consultation I decided that I couldn't, in good conscience, provide this service. I explained to her that I couldn't guarantee that her hair would be blonde or be healthy by the end of the treatment.

I went into further detail, explaining my reasoning. I explained that because I had never worked on her hair, I had no indication it would lift out properly. Sometimes when pulling the red pigment out of certain hair types, the underlying pigments of orange and yellow become pervasive. It's impossible to achieve a true blonde without bleaching the crap out it. She'd be left with damage hair that was difficult to manage.

I held my boundary and told her I wouldn't compromise her

---

hair. She resisted and pushed the color treatment. Because I held firm, she left the salon in frustration.

At a coffee shop later that day I ran into the red-headed woman, she pulled me aside to thank me for my honesty and integrity. She'd had time to think about why I said no and could appreciate that I was trying to do a good job.

By making these lists, you can start to create boundaries that allow for more flow. To help you understand how this might work, let's explore ways I have used boundaries to illuminate or avoid particular BLOCK items.

For example, I began building a larger clientele so I didn't have gaps in my schedule. To do this, I also needed to work on my technical limitations like military cuts and curly hair. I worked on these by taking a class and practicing these skills.

I also decided I needed a boundary to avoid feeling stressed at work. I made it clear that I would only work a maximum of 6 days a week. If I had to work a Sunday, I would take another day off. I've learned that if I don't have at least one day off a week, I get irritable, tired, and lose focus.

Another boundary I demarcated is to never consume alcohol. I am a person who can't handle alcohol. It compromises my effectiveness at work. I use it in unhealthy ways to deal with stress. And I make incredibly poor decisions when I drink. I decided drinking had no place in my life.

Just like life, your boundaries will fluctuate and change over time. As you continue to build a path toward what you want, your boundaries will evolve too. It's important to keep track of your progress and celebrate your successes. Over the next week, check in with your list and see if you are straying from your boundaries. If you find yourself out of alignment with your goals, recommit to holding your boundaries. It shows respect for yourself and for others.

There are three additional points you should keep in mind as you work through this exercise. These address issues you'll inevitably encounter as you begin setting and holding your boundaries.

Why Worry?

There may be items on your lists that are difficult to approach, or that are out of your control altogether. For instance, you can never control other people's behavior. For the stressors in your life that you cannot control, there is only one course of action—acceptance.

Before I understood this concept, I would get quite cranky when there was a last-minute cancellation at the salon. All day I'd feel surly and irritable. Until, one day, I realized there was one thing I could do about the situation—I could control how I felt about it. Instead wasting time and energy feeling angry, I use this free time to catch up on my social media accounts, clean my tools, and help my fellow co-workers. It was incredibly liberating to recognize that I couldn't control my client's behavior, but I could control how I reacted to them. I *did* have options: I could let my emotions control me. Or I could take charge of my emotions and do something productive.

Accepting what you cannot control is hard. But learning to relax into these moments is essential. Otherwise you'll drive yourself mad. If you can practice acceptance, life becomes much easier.

For example, instead of worrying about paying the bills, I switched the way I was thinking about the situation by saying: "I accept I am doing everything in my power to feel financially comfortable, while also taking action to become more finically stable."

In certain situations, it can be hard to recognize if you actually have a choice. Here's an illustration to help you recognize when something is within your control. I call it my "Why Worry" test:

Life will never be stress free. You may continue to sweat the small stuff from time to time. You will always have areas you'll want to improve upon as well as find opportunities for growth. But remember: treat yourself with kindness. It's okay to accept the things that are outside of our control.

Why Worry
Illustration

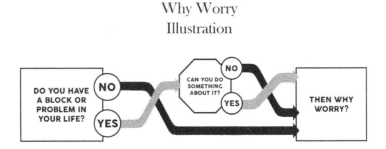

Learn to Say No

Another skill you'll need when creating and maintaining boundaries is the ability to say *no*. Learning to say *no* brings integrity into your life. It will help you cultivate clients, customers, and people that support your desired life.

Let me give you an example: Learning to say *no* to certain clients has allowed me to focus on those clients that create flow for me. Remember the woman who wanted blonde hair for her friend's wedding? I had a choice: I could provide a service I felt uncomfortable with, risking the integrity of her hair and my reputation. Or I could accept a little discomfort and be honest with her and say *no*. I was protecting her hair and my reputation. Because I said *no*, she recognized I did it out of respect.

But it's not enough to just say *no*. In order to hold your ground, it's also important to explain why. Not only did I tell this client *no*, I gave her an explanation of why I refused to provide the service. I explained that it was my job to care for her hair. This includes maintaining the health and integrity of her hair and making sure she felt confident managing her style at home. I explained that if I tried to strip the pigment from her hair so she could go blonde, I wasn't doing my job. And, in the end, I knew she would be unhappy with the result.

Saying no and explaining why gives you credibility. If I were working at a makeup counter and someone picked out a foundation color and I knew wouldn't look good on them, I would explain why it wouldn't look good. If I simply said, "Oh that color will make you look awful!" It might come across as rude and, perhaps, make me look like I'm not knowledgeable. If I explain why, it helps the other person understand my motivation and supports my value system. If I said, "That color will not work for you because it's too dark for your complexion. You'll need something slightly lighter, let me help you get a color closer to your skin type." I said no, gave them a reason why, and created an alternative solution that solved their makeup concerns.

Sometimes it's good to move your boundaries. If a friend wants me to go to a concert and I know I will be out later than my boundaries allow, I have to weigh the benefits of breaking my boundary and the benefits of staying committed. There will be times in your life when you need to realign your boundaries. That's okay! Boundaries are guidelines that allow you to operate at your full potential. Sometimes new opportunities arise. Be aware enough to take advantage of them.

But, if you are moving boundaries for experiences or situations that do not elevate or support your goals, you need to step back and reevaluate. Breaking boundaries shows a lack of respect. It allows feelings of doubt and shame to muddy your path and hinder your progress.

The Cost of Boundaries

After a period of staying true to your patterns and boundaries you may begin to lose certain clients and friends. While this may feel unsettling at first, it just means you are realigning your personal and professional relationships so they support your goals. Your patterns and boundaries are opening up new opportunities; you are designing the life you want.

Slowly, as I stopped drinking, I realized I was loosing touch with particular friends. They were my "bar buddies." All we had in common was drinking. Once I eliminated the drinking, those people slowly faded out of my life.

I noticed this happening at work too. When I set new boundaries at work, I lost a few clients. I had a client who was always twenty minutes late for his appointment. I decided to institute a policy that anyone who was more than fifteen minutes late for an appointment would need to reschedule. After this client was forced to reschedule a few times, he found a different hairstylist who tolerated his constant tardiness. But I realized this was a good thing. I wasn't rushing to catch up all day, compromising other clients' time with me. I began attracting clients who had respect for my time because I respected and valued their time.

When you hold to your boundaries, it may seem that it comes at a cost. But boundaries only show people that you deserve respect. And in return, boundaries attract people who are willing to give you that respect.

RECAP:

Boundaries are your limits, a line in the sand you draw and will not cross. Boundaries allow us to be successful and make room for growth.

Define your job, and then do it!

Identify things in your personal and professional life that put you in a state of flow, happiness, or wellbeing. Identify things that seem to create roadblocks, frustration, or stress in your personal and professional life.

Set boundaries to encourage more things that create flow in your life.

Acknowledge situations you have no control over. Follow the Why Worry diagram.

Saying no shows integrity.

Boundaries help cultivate healthy relationship at home and work.

Chapter 4 Self-care
Daily habits for success

"If your compassion does not include yourself, it is incomplete." —Jack Kornfield

Self-care is exactly what it sounds like—taking care of number one. This may sound selfish, but you really can't expect to be better and do better without taking care of yourself. And you certainly can't help other people if you're neglecting your own needs.

In 1943 Abraham Maslow published a paper called *A Theory of Human Motivation*. In this paper, he lays out a theory now known as Maslow's Hierarchy of Needs. It explains why taking care of yourself is essential. It is the backbone for understanding your needs and creating a system of self-care.

To understanding Maslow's theory, think of your needs as a pyramid with five different levels. (The bottom two levels are basic needs. The middle two are psychological needs. And the top level is self-fulfillment.)

Maslow's Hierarchy of Needs

The bottom section of the pyramid houses our physiological needs. They include things like food, water, shelter, and rest. They are basic needs for survival.

Next, comes our need for safety. This includes things like personal security, emotional security, financial security as well as health and wellbeing.

Then comes social belonging. This includes intimate relationships, friendships, and family connections.

The fourth tier represents our self-esteem needs—feelings of accomplishments, confidence, and self-respect.

Lastly, at the top of the pyramid, is self-actualization. This is a desire to achieve our full potential. This includes showcasing your abilities and talents, pursuing goals and seeking happiness.

This hierarchy illustrates our universal human needs, things we all must attain in order to grow and progress. This system of needs is designed to work from the bottom up. To achieve self-fulfillment, one must first meet the needs below it. We cannot achieve our esteem needs if our social belonging, safety, or basic physiological needs are not met. The foundation must be stable before we can begin constructing the house above it. Recognizing that we are all motivated by our needs helps us take better care of ourselves and others. It is a path toward empathy and compassion, not selfishness.

Creating Self-Care

To be the best that we can be, we have to take care of ourselves. We must have our basic needs met before we can begin trying to meet the needs of others. This chapter focuses on creating daily habits that elevate and sustain growth.

Story Time!

Shortly after I turned 21, I did what a lot of people do when they turn 21—"tie one on."

I went to a fundraiser for a local non-profit, and the whole night I made sure my glass was never empty.

I got home around 1:00 a.m., and had to be to work at 8:00 a.m. My first appointment that day was a new client. I proceeded with her consultation and began the service. It was a simple haircut and style.

You can probably guess what happened next. As I began blow-drying her hair, a wave of nausea hit me like a hammer in the face. I began sweating profusely.

I turned the blow drier off, set it down gently, and told her I needed to blow my nose. I was in the bathroom for ten minutes throwing up.

I have never been so hung over (or embarrassed) in my entire life!

I cleaned myself up and got back to my client. She asked if everything was okay. I lied and said, "It's my damn allergies, I'm so sorry about that."

She knew what was going on. She knew I didn't have allergies and probably heard me throwing up. Needless to say, I never saw her in the salon again.

Daily self-care habits are patterns that we create in order to operate at our full potential. They will be unique to you and your life situation. But I've found seven areas of focus that help make it easier to get your hierarchy of needs met. These seven key daily practices have helped me become more present in my own life. They have allowed me to create healthy patterns and boundaries while assisting me in becoming more empathic and compassionate with my clients and those I encounter. We will explore creating healthy patterns and boundaries for each of these seven areas in order to elevate yourself and perform at your peak in any given situation.

The seven practices are food, water, movement, meditation, sunshine, respect and love.

Food: You are what you eat.

What I'm about to say may sound glib, but it's true. You have to eat well to do well. Maintaining a proper diet helps regulate how you feel mentally, physically and emotionally.

For example, if you consume large amounts of caffeine or sugar, your body is going to get quite cranky. After the sugar or caffeine high wears off, you'll be left feeling irritable, fatigued, disoriented and depressed. Likewise, if you're not eating a balance of fruits, vegetables, carbohydrates, and proteins you're likely feeling these same symptoms.

I'm not here to tell you what you should and shouldn't eat. I'm just here to help you become a little more aware of what you put into your body. Awareness is the first step in making change. (If you need more information on how to develop healthy eating habits, refer to my list of resources at the end or the book.)

What I do want to offer are two tips for cultivating better eating habits:

The first is to listen to your own body. If it doesn't make you feel good, don't eat it. If you are unsure about what foods make you feel good and what don't, start a food journal. Over a two-week period, write down everything you eat. Afterward, evaluate and isolate the foods that give you a sense of health and wellbeing and those that have possible side effects. If you're still unsure, keep journaling until you've found foods/menu items that help you feel your best. For example, after a lot of trial and error, I switched to a vegetarian diet because eating vegetables, fruits and plant protein just makes me feel better.

The next tip I'd like to offer is to make time for regular meals. This can be challenging in our fast-paced world, but the rewards outweigh the hassle of sticking to a regular schedule. Finding a set time to eat creates an internal pattern or rhythm for your body. It helps with digestion and regulates blood-sugar levels, which keeps your energy level consistent. Eating at random times of the day or skipping meals taxes your energy, creates imbalances in your body, messes with your moods and wreaks havoc with your metabolism. I've found that if I eat breakfast at 7 or 8 a.m., lunch between 12 and 1 p.m., and dinner around 6 or 7 p.m., I have enough energy throughout the day to function at my best.

NOTE: As a hairdresser, I know it can be challenging to find time for a lunch break. But if you're diligent about booking yourself out for 30 minutes everyday at the same time, you'll save yourself from feeling crappy at the end of the day. Even though you could be making money during that lunch break, it's not worth the risks to your health and wellbeing. Plus, you'll have more energy to devote to your clients. They'll love the attention and want to come back to you more often.

Water: Are you drinking enough water?

Staying hydrated is an easy way to avoid chronic ailments like muscle soreness, headaches, migraines, back pain, dry skin, lack of energy, irritability, and unexplained hunger. (If you find yourself hungry all day, it could be a sign that you're not getting enough water.)

There are some easy ways to determine if you are drinking enough water throughout the day. Let's start with 8 x 8—drink 8 ounces of water 8 times a day. It's a useful tool to monitor your water consumption. One note of caution: this may not be enough water if you consume caffeine, if you are outside for long periods of the day or do a lot of endurance exercises. Try adding another 8-ounce cup of water if you drink a lot of coffee. If you exercise, add a few extra cups of water. And remember, if you feel thirsty, you're already dehydrated.

Another way to determine how much water you need is to take your weight and divide it by two; the answer is the amount of water you should drink in ounces. For example, I weigh 165 pounds. Divide that by 2 and I'm supposed to drink 82.5 ounces of water a day. (I shoot for around 126 ounces because of my physical activity and I drink a few cups of coffee throughout the day.)

An easy way to develop the habit of drinking enough water is to carry around a water bottle wherever you go. Having water handy encourages you to sip it throughout the day. Plus, it gives you a simple way to keep track of how much you've had. I know if I have to refill my water bottle twice in a day, I'm getting what I need. (Sip your water, and avoid chugging. It just gives you a stomachache.)

Now, to keep yourself honest about how much water you drink in a day, I recommend you take out the old journal again. Work out the math for your personal water consumption, and for extra credit, record how much you actually drink in a day. You may choose the 8 x 8 method or the weight method. Either way, find a realistic goal that works for you.

Movement: What keeps you going?

I hear people say, "I want to exercise, but I just don't have the time." I get it. It takes time and effort. But engaging in regular exercise improves so many aspects of your life that you really can't afford not to get up and move. This doesn't mean you have to become a marathon runner. There are a lot of options to explore. Sports like biking, tennis, softball, or basketball are great group activities. Taking a dance, yoga or kickboxing class can help you find motivation. Everyone is different. Just find something that works for you and your body. It may be as simple as waking up thirty minutes earlier to take a walk.

20 minutes of physical activity every day benefits your body, brain, and mind. It strengthens muscles and bones, improves balance and coordination, and it boosts memory, learning and cognitive function. It's also an effective treatment for a wide range of disorders such as depression, insomnia, anxiety and ADHD.

My parents run a small business. They manage all their employees, maintain relationships with their accounts, and enjoy a fulfilling home life. A few years ago they made it a priority to start taking time for exercise. They wake up every morning at 6 a.m. to take a walk in the park. Within a year, they lost weight, had more energy, and felt an overall better sense of wellbeing. Now they both go to the gym daily and still walk around the park.

My parents started with something small and worked their way up. You don't have to run out and buy a gym membership that you may or may not use. Find something that fits your lifestyle and interests. For me, I've never loved going to the gym. It's hard to stay motivated to exercise when you don't like what you are doing. Instead of dragging myself to the gym, I decided to try rock climbing and yoga and found they suit my body and lifestyle better. My point is just try new things until you find something you enjoy.

For those of us in the service industry, it's also important to find ways to prevent or alleviate repetitive stress injuries. As a certified yoga instructor, I've adopted a few practices that assist me behind the chair. These postures are designed to get my body moving in a way that counteracts how I hold my body as I work in the salon. I practice these postures everyday to help prevent the injuries hairstylists tend to get like rounding back, shoulder pain, carpal tunnel, aching legs and feet. (For more information on how to prevent injuries at work, check the reference section at the end of the book.)

Meditation: Come back to yourself.

Sit down and enjoy the silence. Mediation is a wonderful tool to use daily. This ancient practice has been used to help focus the mind and bring awareness. The mind and body are not separate but one. Meditation is an excellent way to access the positive affects of this brain-body connection. It benefits your heart, endocrine system and immune system while counteracting chronic pain, anxiety, depression, and stress.

For most of us, our minds are forced to race from one thought to the next. Our brains are constantly planning, problem solving, predicting and practicing. While cutting someone's hair I'll be thinking about what I'm going to make for dinner, what emails I need to respond to, rehearsing my schedule for the week and so on. Sometimes it's important to let all that go, to rest your mind and quiet your thoughts. Resting your mind regularly helps bring clarity and perspective when you need it most, during times of stress and overwhelm.

Meditation helps you to become more present in your thoughts, feelings and actions throughout your day. If you are having trouble mediating, there are podcasts, YouTube videos and an endless variety of books that can further assist you. At the back of this book I have provided some resources and a few simple meditation practices to assist you in your practice. I invite you to start a daily practice of just 5 minutes a day, you'll be amazed by how those few minutes can shift your day and perspective.

Sunshine: Let the rays fall down.

Getting a daily dose of Vitamin D from the sun is very important. Experts say that you should get at least 15 minutes a day in the sun to get a healthy dose of Vitamin D. Vitamin D is important because it makes us happy. Not getting enough sunshine can cause seasonal depression and other harmful side effects. Make time in your day to get in the sun and get your daily dose of Vitamin D. If you can't get outside as much as you'd like, you might want to talk to your family doctor about taking a Vitamin D supplement.

Respect: If you look good, you'll feel good.

Looking good on the outside reflects how you feel on the inside. When I wake up on the wrong side of the bed, I know it's time to find an outfit that makes me feel better. I know from experience that if I feel good about how I look, it will reflect throughout the rest of my day.

That's why I came up with a few tips to boost your self-confidence. The first is dress to feel your best. This might mean wearing something to work that you feel powerful, sexy and confident in. Or it could be you save your comfy clothes for relaxing at home. (I say this while wearing my baggy harem pants.) We all want to feel comfortable in our clothes, but sweatpants are only helping you at the gym and perhaps before you go to bed. Showing up for work or at an event in lounge pants sends the wrong message. (Let's be honest, no one gets laid or hired while wearing gym clothes or holey sweatpants.) Being aware of how your outfit pairs with your daily activities will not only make you look good but it'll make you feel confident.

The next tip is to schedule a weekend to go through your closet. Try on all your clothing; see what fits and what doesn't. Take some time to hone-in on your style. If there are pieces of clothing you haven't worn in the last year, it's time to let them go.

The last piece of advice I'd like to offer is about style. Fashion is fleeting, trends come and go, but style is unique to you. As a hairstylist I am adamant about helping people find their individual style. If you need help with working out how you want to present yourself to the world, here a few tools you can access:

Pintrest is a great resource for inspiration.

Talk to your hairstylist about haircuts and grooming techniques that works for your face, body, and skin complexion.

Go to a department store and have a personal shopper help pick out outfits. Check out the online retailers like asos.com.

Love: Love yourself daily.

Rupaul, drag queen superstar, says, "If you can't love yourself, how the hell are you going to love somebody else!" Truer words have never been spoken. Take a moment everyday to show love and compassion towards yourself. Do something for you, and only you. Spend quality time with yourself.

This could mean you treat yourself to something nice, take yourself out for dinner, or see a movie. You could take time out of your day for a nice long bath, go on a hike, cook a nice dinner, or give yourself a facial. This may sound bizarre, but taking time to show yourself some love is important. It helps you re-energize so you are better equipped to empathize when other people need a little love too.

Putting it Together

It's remarkable how making positive shifts in your daily self-care routines can help you achieve your goals, improve your relationships and help you grow at work and as an individual.

Taking care of yourself is the best way to start taking better care of your customers. It took me years to find a formula of daily self-care that worked for me. Nothing happened overnight. Change was slow, but it did happen. It's important to remind yourself that creating new patterns take patience.

Take one step at a time. It's perfectly acceptable to focus on diet and water consumption for a month. Then add in some movement exercises for another 30 days. Then add your meditation practice, and so on. Add one step every month. Pretty soon your daily habits and patterns will be transformed.

Trying to change all your patterns overnight just leads to frustration and burnout. Take these steps gradually and at a comfortable pace. Be patient and enjoy the journey.

Writing Exercise: Document Your Progress

Writing out your intentions is a great way to hold yourself accountable. As part of your daily self-care routine, use your journal to track your progress: write out a weekly meal plan, track what and when you eat, track your water consumption, brainstorm ideas for new activities, list resources from this book you want to check out, make plans for your wardrobe, and think of something fun you'd like to treat yourself to. Make this journal your own. You can take monthly photos and add them to document your progress. Find inspirational quotes to help keep you motivated. Or just use it to clear your mind and dump all your thoughts onto a page.

Remember, there are three stages to making change—think about it, say it (or write it), and act upon it. Writing about your self-care habits will encourage you to act upon your goals. Later, you can look back at your journal entries and feel proud of how much you've accomplish.

Remember, getting your needs met is not selfish. It's the best way to care for yourself so you can care for others at work and at home.

RECAP:

Maslow's Hierarchy of Needs: Physiological, Safety, Love/Belong, Esteem, and Self-Actualization.

7 daily habits to be aware of, the food you eat, the amount of water you consume, exercise, meditate, get some sun, and love yourself.

Change your habits one at a time not all at once; this will help you maintain your new habits.

Take your time when creating new habits, no need to rush it all.

Document your progress.

Chapter 5 Empathy

Understanding and cultivating empathy

"When two people relate to each other authentically and humanly, God is the electricity that surges between them." —Brené Brown

There will be moments in your career that will push your boundaries. Like a bamboo shoot in a ferocious storm, we have to learn to be flexible and bend with nature and not resist the troubles of life. Resistance causes tension and invariably leads us to snap.

This chapter contains information that will help you when dealing with the emotions of those you encounter, especially your clients. The skills learned here will assist you in creating connection as well as maintaining your boundaries.

To navigate through challenging or emotional conversations or interactions, we must experience, cultivate and understand empathy. Before we get into too much depth, we need to understand and define empathy and learn how it's different from sympathy.

Empathy is the ability to understand and share the feelings of another person, while sympathy is expressing pity or sorrow for another person. Empathy is sharing what another person is feeling. Empathy is simply listening and acknowledging. Empathy creates connection. It is the key to understanding other people. Striving towards empathy builds better, healthier relationships.

Sympathy means you remain on the outside looking in, not fully embracing or experiencing the moment. Sympathy is disconnected. It maintains barriers.

Story Time!

I had a unique experience with a client. We'll call her Samantha. I've known Samantha for a few years now, and she's been having a rough time this last year.

One day she was in the salon getting her hair colored. While I was applying the color, she received a phone call. Moments later, she hung up the phone. She was white as a sheet and speechless.

"Is everything okay?" I asked. Her eyes welled with tears. She proceeded to tell me that her daughter, who is pregnant, was hospitalized the day before. The phone call was from her son-in-law, informing her that they had lost the baby. They were 7 months pregnant. This couple had struggled to conceive. It was utterly devastating.

In that moment, I knew there was only one choice—I had to be present for her grief. There was nothing I could do to fix the situation. Nothing I could say would ever alleviate her sadness. All I could do was simply listen and acknowledge the pain, the sadness she was experiencing.

"That is awful. I hear your sadness. I am here with you," I said.

Everyone has the right to feel his or her emotions—happiness, sadness, grief, joy—whatever they may be. And we all need to feel like our feelings matter. When those around you take a moment to experience the world as you do, you both become better human beings. This doesn't mean you have to hold the same values or maintain the same beliefs. It simply means you have the capacity to understand.

Saying "I'm here with you" implies you are there, in the moment, acknowledging someone else's experience.

Empathy is not about giving advice, trying to fix a problem, or put a silver lining on a bad situation. Empathy can be practiced in alignment with your boundaries. Remember, we are not therapists, we are cosmetologists.

Deep listening

Dr. Brené Brown is one of my favorite authors. You may know her from her Ted Talks—*Listening to Shame* and *The Power of Vulnerability*. She is also a genius when it comes to empathy. She believes we all have the capacity to be more empathic. And we achieve this with deep listening.

Deep listening is when you truly listen to what another other person is saying. This means listening without the need to fix a problem or control the conversation. It is listening without judgment or shame.

It sounds simple, but deep listening takes practice. Deep listening takes all of your focus. You can't really listen to someone while you are thinking about what you're going to make for dinner, or formulating a point you want to make when they finish. Deep listening means you take in every word. Your mind and body are focused on the other person, listening as you process and take in the information.

Let's break down the two key aspects of deep listening—listening and responding. This may seem elementary but stick with me.

Step 1: Listen.

While listening to someone you are not thinking about how you will respond. You are not anticipating when you get to say something. You are simply listening to them, taking in every word. You listen free of judgment and free of shame. (When you are judging or shaming someone you cannot really hear what is being said. Judgment and shame only makes us feel better about our own insecurities.)

Step 2: Respond.

First, one must be genuine in your listening. The way you respond or react while someone else is talking can validate that you are really listening. These are nonverbal cues—nodding your head, making eye contact, and then commenting only when they are finished speaking.

Next, you respond by giving a brief restatement of what you heard. You are not here to fix a problem. That diminishes their emotions and what they are experiencing. It can actually make a person feel worse about their situation. React by recognizing and acknowledging their emotions and ensure they understand that you are there with them.

Being empathic and cultivating deep listening skills creates connections. Having these skills will allow you to connect with your client on an emotional level without dragging you into the story and making their experience yours.

Boundaries and Empathy

It is vitally important to hold boundaries around empathy. If we have no boundaries, we leave ourselves vulnerable to other people's emotional baggage. If you are feeling overwhelming dread, unavoidable sadness, anger, or perhaps feelings of helplessness with certain clients, it could be a sign your boundaries are being breached.

To avoid taking on the stories and the emotions of others, I recommend these tips and tricks to re-establish healthy boundaries while being truly empathetic. These can be practiced anytime and anywhere.

Shake it off:

Start by shaking it off! After listening to a client's experience, I like to step into a private room and shake my hands and arms, shaking off the experience and emotions that may have attached themselves to my current state of being. Also, washing your hands or face is a therapeutic way of metaphorically cleansing the experience from your body. It allows for a clean slate as you take on your next client. If you are a visual person, close your eyes while washing your hands and imagine the emotional baggage is washing away.

Write it off:

If you go home still thinking about a conversation you had with someone, journal about it. The best way to process information and other people's emotions is to express your experience. By writing it down, you process the experience while expressing your thoughts and feelings around the matter.

Talk it off:

If all else fails, seek a professional to help process the information. I see a therapist once a month. Talking to a professional about your experiences can help you process them in healthy ways. Having a therapist or counselor can be your best tool in navigating through difficult clients and intense emotional experiences. Finding a good therapist is like finding a good hairdresser—it may take time to find

someone that is a good fit. A great resource is
www.psychologytoday.com

Listen to Yourself

Deep listening doesn't just apply to others; it also applies when listening to yourself. A clouded mirror can't reflect the truth. You have to get good at stilling you mind so you can pick up on what your body is telling you. Do your own emotional healing work, pay attention to triggers, listen to yourself first before you take someone else's advice. You'll be in a better position to listen to others if you are taking care of yourself. Don't deny your body and mind the care it needs and deserves.

Story Time!

Sometimes I'm not very good at listening to my body. Not too long ago I went to the climbing gym for an hour, then to a yoga class, and later that afternoon taught a hair styling class.

Needless to say, I pushed myself too hard. Halfway through my class I began experiencing horrible pain in my right shoulder. I pushed through the pain and finished the class. The following day I woke up and the pain was worse!

I scheduled an appointment with the chiropractor, but unfortunately that didn't help. I had to go to work that afternoon. I was patient and aware of my limitations that day and did the best not to stress out my shoulder. The next day the pain was still there, and I was able to see a medical massage therapist. She worked on my body for two hours and by the end she said to take it easy, ice my shoulder and not to exert it in the next few days. I finally listened to my body. I avoided climbing and yoga for an entire week. I was a bit frustrated, but the injury healed. I'm glad I listened.

Writing Exercise: Listening to Yourself

Write in your journal daily. Commit to writing every day for a week. (You could also challenge yourself to write for 30 days.) Do this exercise first thing in the morning or before you go to bed at night.

Throughout the week, write down what you are feeling. Look inward as you write and listen to yourself. Write what your body is telling you. If you are feeling really happy, write it down. If you have body aches, write it down and be specific. The point is to listen to your mind and body. Write it down without judgment. For example, recently I wrote in my journal: "Today I am struggling, here is why..." and proceeded to write why I was struggling. I felt unmotivated, and in a rut creatively. I didn't try to fix the problem. First, I just acknowledged what I was feeling. After the acknowledgment, then I began looking at what patterns I was holding on to. I eventually found new patterns to spark my creativity again.

If you are having physical pains, write them down, "Today my shoulder hurts, it made it difficult for me to round-brush hair today. I will go home and ice my shoulder, rest, and practice exercises before and after work to stretch out and relax my shoulder." Acknowledge the physical sensations in your body just as much as the emotional sensations.

Throughout the day, our bodies are constantly communicating to us and trying to give us information. If you clench your teeth and tighten your jaw, what is your body trying to tell you? If you have a certain customer that comes into work and the sight of them makes your stomach wrench up, what is your body telling you? Stop, listen, and respond. The same principles of deep listening apply to you as much as they do when you are listening to others. Truly listen, don't make up stories about yourself, don't shame yourself, and don't judge yourself—simply listen.

Listening Creates Patterns

Let's tie in everything up to this point:

Recognize your patterns.

Create boundaries based off of your patterns.

Develop a system of self-care.

Cultivate empathy and deep listening.

When we follow this path, our bodies will give us vital information—signals that circle back to where our boundaries are being pushed too far. We then start the cycle over again, refining our path toward a better life and career by change the patterns that no longer facilitate growth.

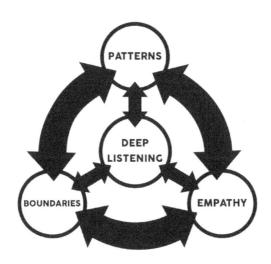

Deep listening is the street that connects us to life. Utilizing empathy and deep listening keeps us in a place of peace, love, understanding, compassion, and connection. This isn't a recipe for total bliss. But if practiced daily, it can help you avoid misunderstandings with others and foster personal growth.

RECAP:

Empathy is the ability to understand and share the feelings of another person. Sympathy is expressing pity or sorrow with another person.

Deep listening: learn to listen to others and respond by acknowledging their emotions.

Practice deep listening skills on yourself.

Write about yourself. Check in daily and write about the sensations you are experiencing. Journal about thoughts, feelings, and physical pains.

Patterns, boundaries, empathy, and deep listening all affect one another and support each other.

Deep listening allows us to stay connected with the world and approach life from a place of love, compassion, and understanding.

Chapter 6 Ego

Our friend, our enemy

"The ego is not the master in its own house."

—Sigmund Freud

As we begin cultivating better, healthier patterns and operate within a system of self-care, there are many challenges. Nevertheless, there is one challenge that is universally tricky—taking control of your ego before it takes control of you.

When I first stepped into my career as a hairdresser at the ripe old age of 19, I was quite confident I knew everything about the world. Like most people at this age, I was cocky, arrogant and blessed with an ego the size of Texas. I was never wrong. I was better than most. And I could brag like nobody's business about the amazing opportunities and experiences I was having. I was also miserable, lonely, and jealous of every one else's success. There isn't enough money in the world to convince me to go back to being 19.

Over the years, I have developed a more genuine sense of self, and I have found strategies to keep my ego in check. I've learned that when I get an anxious knot in the back of my brain, when I start comparing myself to other people, my ego is trying to push me around and complicate my life.

You're probably wondering why this is important? Why talk about ego? The simple truth is that understanding your own ego can help you make better decisions.

Everyone has an ego. It's formed by the beliefs we acquire throughout our lifetime. True or not, these beliefs perpetuate a self-image and form your identity. Once established, your ego doesn't like being messed with. It comes up with all kinds of creative ways to protect itself. Thoughts like "I'm better than you!" or "Nobody likes me!" are indications that your ego is trying to shift the plot because it's feeling threatened. If these thoughts begin to dictate how you react to people and situations, that's when you have a problem.

Because the concept of ego is so complex, let's explore what an out-of-control ego looks like. An overly aggressive ego seeks approval and validation at all costs. Its only concern is to be right (to preserve your current construct of who you think you are). Similarly, ego resists against change, helpful feedback and collaboration. These are some classic sign that your ego is out of control and driving your decision-making:

You enjoy gossiping about other people's flaws.

You can't back down from a heated debate until you feel you have won the argument.

You compare yourself to other people who you feel are better than you (better looking, more intelligent, happier, wealthier).

You compare yourself to other people who you feel are not as good as you (less intelligent, lower status).

You feel jealous when other people do well.

You constantly talk about yourself and never invite other people to share.

You are driven to win rather than doing your best.

You sulk when you don't "win" (as apposed to feeling proud that you did your best).

You set impossible goals and beat yourself up when you don't reach them.

You blame other people when things don't go your way.

Over time your ego can collect a surplus of misguided beliefs about who you are and what you're good at. It can wreak havoc with your identity. Without some level of self-awareness, your ego can trap you in a cycle of self-imposed melodrama, it can shut you off from connection, and it can leave you feeling stuck with choices you have no control over.

Ego, The Best Storyteller

The ego is quite good at betraying us. It likes to wrap itself up in comparison and invest in stories that have no connection to reality. It likes to perpetuate narratives like:

"I am not good enough."

"I am not likeable."

"I am not deserving."

These stories color our perceptions about the world and ourselves. Layer upon layer, story upon story, these destructive tales cripple your personal identity. Ego, like a virus in the body, can infect healthy systems with false statements that alter your reality. These stories manifest in the form of thoughts and perceptions of your past and future, and show up in your interactions with people and your reactions to events. They can paralyze you from taking action.

Stories are fine, but that's all they are—just stories. I think about all the time I've wasted attending to some of these erroneous stories—being jealous of another's success; blaming and shaming myself for trying my best and still failing; obsessing about some absurd thing I said to a client, friend, co-worker, or date; the list goes on. With all the time I've wasted on telling myself stories, I could have taken a pottery class!

To see what holding on to our ego's stories does, here is an experiment you can try: Get a glass of water, stand and hold it for ten minutes without resting your arm or putting the glass down. Holding the glass may not bother you at first, but after a few minutes your arm begins to get tired. As more time passes, you may begin to fidget and become restless. And once you get close to the ten-minute mark, your arm will feel heavy, tired, and all out exhausted. This is what stories do to your mind and body. The longer your ego holds on to the past, the creative fiction, the self-doubt, and so on, the more tired, fatigued, and drained you become These stories keep you trapped inside a nasty loop and prevent you from enjoying a present full of possibility and promise.

The Ego as Our Friend

Don't get me wrong, ego isn't a menacing overlord that lives in your head, waiting to cut you down. Ego is just a collection of beliefs. It is the source of your self-esteem and self-image. Problems only arise when that self-image is negative, inaccurate, or even overly positive. When a client gives you a compliment like "I love my haircut!" or leaves a very generous tip, it can be quite an ego boost. Ego isn't a terrible monster that needs to be destroyed and eliminated. I view it as child that needs to be taught how to behave so it doesn't throw a fit every time it has to eat broccoli.

Your ego can be the driving force that pushes you in a new direction or shows you the way to a profound experience. When I first started writing this book, I was afraid to talk about it. Feelings of inadequacy and self-doubt circled me like buzzards. Fortunately, I was able to sidestep these thoughts long enough to share what I was doing. Once I opened up, the response was invigorating. There were people who wanted to hear what I had to say. My ego flipped its script and said, "Oh! I like this feeling. People are interested in my work. Let's see what's next!"

Most of us just need some time to get a different perspective. Instead of letting your story-telling ego keep you prisoner, take a moment to move outside of the story. (This is where having an awareness of your ego comes in handy.) Ask yourself, "Is this really true? Am I really not good, likeable or deserving enough to try or accomplish
?"

It's healthy to recognize you have imperfections, but you don't need to death spiral into them. When you notice feelings of negativity (or superiority) taking root, step outside of yourself for a bit of self-reflection. Here are some key actions to practice:

Love yourself as you are, flaws and all.

Admit when you are wrong.

Find contentment in where you are in life.

Understand that feelings of unworthiness are nothing but stories.

Don't let jealousy drive your decisions.

Be proud of your accomplishments and share them without a need for validation from others.

Do your best and understand that it's okay to make mistakes.

Accept that you don't always have to win.

Set goals and be open to the possibility that they might change as you progress in life.

Take ownership of your life.

Story Time!

When we feel hurt or attacked, the ego's first response is to protect itself. Usually it's at the expense of other people.

As a stylist, I've encountered (like every stylist does) situations that hit my ego in the tender parts. I've had clients who— after much work on my part—hate their finished style or feel unsatisfied because it wasn't what they envisioned. It can be a humiliating experience.

Invariably my ego says, "Oh she was never going to be happy, no matter what I did," or "She should have chosen a different color, then she would've liked it." And sometimes my ego goes so far as to say, "Oh, who cares. I didn't like her anyway. I'll be happy if I never see her again."

What's the common factor in all these responses? My ego is trying to place blame on the client. I've learned that if these nasty thoughts start playing out in my head, my ego is in protection mode. It's a cue that I need to take a moment, step outside of myself, and get a different perspective on the situation. It's time to take responsibility. Here is how I try to approach a situation like this (if I'm on my game):

> *I start by taking ownership for what happened. Instead of blaming the client, I own my mistakes. I ask myself, "Wow I screwed up! What went wrong? Why didn't she like her hair? What could I have done differently to ensure her happiness? How can I fix this?" My favorite question is: "What can I learn from this experience?"*
>
> *Then I ask myself if I knew the color or haircut she asked for wouldn't work for her? If I did know, I remind myself I should have communicated this to her (no matter how uncomfortable the conversation would have been).*
>
> *And finally, I try to never let a client leave unhappy! I do everything in my power to make the situation right. This could mean redoing the service or refunding the clients money.*
>
> *None of this is painless. It just helps brings a little self-awareness to the situation. It doesn't make my ego feel better, but it does help me make better choices as I try to remedy the situation or at least learn from my mistakes.*

Picking up on the signs that your ego is out of control isn't always easy. Self-awareness takes time and practice. Nevertheless, self-awareness is the key to cultivating your authentic self (as apposed to an overblown ego). Up to this point, the work you have done in the previous chapters has all been geared toward the three stages of awareness—Think, Say and Act. Bringing awareness to your ego is no different. By using these tools, you can turn your focus inward and start testing some of the unhealthy assumptions you've made about yourself. You'll start asking yourself, "Do I really feel good about myself or is my ego blaming other people so I can feel good about myself?" If you handle situations with openness, honesty and integrity, you are inviting your genuine self to show up. Of course, you still have an ego, we all do, but you'll recognize more quickly when your ego is trying to take control.

Don't Be Afraid to Ask for Help

The out-of-control ego thinks that it can conquer all. It thinks asking for help is a sign of weakness. This notion is just downright false. (Vidal Sassoon didn't build his brand all by himself. He had a wealth of support from fellow hairdressers who believed in what he was doing.) Asking for help is not a sign of weakness—it's a strength.

There have been many times in my career when I've needed the advice, opinion or collaborations of a colleague. These occasions have only made me a better stylist. Asking for help means you are ready to grow your skillset and knowledge as well as provide clients with results that exceed their expectations. Even with this book, I collaborated with an editor, a business couch, a graphic artist, not to mention my friends and family who read chapters and gave me feedback.

Likewise, when it comes to your personal life, asking for help may be the only way to deal with a problem. When I decided to deal with my addiction to alcohol and my feelings of loss, I knew I didn't have the knowledge or tools to be successful on my own. I sought out a therapist for help. It was the best decision of my life.

The out-of-control ego does not want you to seek help from others. But there will be times when you are stuck in a pattern that you just can't kick. It's okay to get help. Don't let your ego hold you back.

Writing Exercise: Cultivate Your Authentic Self

As you look inward and begin scrutinizing your ego, you'll be relying on the same tools we've used in the previous chapters: Think, Say, Act. These tools are incredibly helpful as you wrangle your out-of-control ego. Here is how to start:

Think: Everyone, at one time or another, engages in negative self-talk (saying things like "I'm so stupid!" or "You can't do that!"). When you notice your inner critic saying nasty things, stop, pause and call it out. Ask yourself: "What am I really feeling?" Are you feeling emotions of jealousy? Are you feeling insecure? Do you feel anger toward someone? Take some time to write down in your journal these emotions or feeling. Be specific about the details. Don't let yourself make any evaluations or judgments about what you write. Just focus on getting these thoughts on paper. Take as much time before moving on to the next step.

Say: Next, look through this list of emotions and feelings and choose one to focus on. Then ask yourself: "Is there a different point of view? How could I see the situation differently?" In your journal, articulate what you think happened. Then write down some other possibilities for what might have happened. Ask yourself: "Am I being honest about my feelings?" Write down any thought you have about what might be motivating you to feel the way you are feeling.

Act: Finally, write out a plan for when you notice yourself feeling this same feeling. These actions should hold personal meaning for you. And they should offer a new perspective on the situation. Here is an example: "When I notice myself feeling jealous about_____, I will pull out a picture of my family (or friends, or cats) and say how grateful I am they are in my life." Be specific and be honest!

As you begin exploring the inner workings of your ego, make sure you write about all aspects of your life—the exciting events as well as the day-to-day, the highly emotional experiences as well as the minor annoyances, the positive and the negative. Writing can help you work out your thoughts, feelings, and experiences. It's the perfect sounding board. It not only helps you develop a well-balanced ego but it also prevents you from unloading all your dirty laundry onto your clients or co-workers.

When you write, there is no such thing as a bad question or idea. It's just a tool you can use to explore something new.

RECAP:

Your ego can lead you astray or your ego can help you make better decisions.

The ego is like a child that needs to be taught how to behave.

Develop an awareness of your ego. Look for a different perspective.

Pull yourself out of the stories that your ego tells you. Be in the present moment.

Ask for help when you need it!

Write about your feelings and emotions to get a closer look at your ego.

Chapter 7 Connection

Creating a community

"The fact is that people are good. Give people affection and security, and they will give affection and be secure in their feelings and their behavior."
—Abraham Maslow

We, as human beings, need connection. We're wired to be part of a group. Connections with our family, friends, clients, and the people in our community fill our biological need for belonging. Everyone enjoys feelings of attachment and acceptance as well as someone to talk to and confide in.

Belonging is the third highest human need in Maslow's Hierarchy. Creating connections with other people can serve us in so many ways. It is vital to our wellbeing. Connections are the wellspring of inspiration and motivation. Connecting with other people expands our worldview, establishes trust, builds networks of support, and opens up unexpected opportunities. It affords us feelings of safety and security and is the source of a great deal of fun. Building upon the work you have already completed, let's explore how to establish healthy connection with your family, friends and clients.

First, it's important to understand that creating healthy patterns and a system of self-care lay the foundation for healthy connections. How can you expect to be able to care for other people if you aren't taking care of yourself?

Next, it's said that we grow to become like the 6 people we hang around with the most. It makes sense to give careful consideration to what your values are, to explore what you care most about in life. If you know what your priorities are, you can evaluate if the people surrounding you support your efforts to live the life you want. You can ask, "Are the people in my life helping me grow into the individual I want to be?" "Does my community support my values?" Look around you—what impact is your environment having on you and your sense of wellbeing?

And finally, the key to forming healthy connections with other people is the ability to look inward. To create deep connections with others, you need to understand yourself first. If you can articulate your values, if you know your strengths and weaknesses, if you are aware of the things that elevate and hinder you, and if you care for your body and mind, your interactions in the world will be guided by empathy, awareness and emotional stability. Then you will be able to nurture connections with people who are in harmony with your integrity and your belief system.

All the work accomplished up to this point has been to gain self-awareness for the purpose of developing useful patterns and letting go of self-destructive beliefs. Now it's time to use your skills of inward reflection and direct the work outward. Take every opportunity to bring awareness to your interactions with people. Bring empathy, love and respect with you as you communicate, cooperate and socialize with people. Don't let your ego color your perceptions and dictate your actions. And, most importantly, seek out communities and networks of support using your values and beliefs as a guide.

Remember, you have a lot to offer the world. If you need help finding connections, look for communities, networks, or groups with a shared purpose and a broader perspective. Think about the things you enjoy—activities, things you are interested in learning, things you want to teach or share. Here are possible places you might want to investigate:

Interest specific groups (book clubs, writing groups, art groups, political groups, etc.)

Volunteer groups

Sports or recreation groups

School or industry organizations

Spiritual or religious groups

At the end of the day, you'll want to find connections that add layers to your life. You'll want to find places that encourage you to grow as an individual. This is true for all relationships—professional relationships, family relationships and intimate relationships.

A Word about Volunteering

The best way to understand true connection and build a broader community is to volunteer. Offering your time, energy, talents and focus to other people opens up opportunities for growth you can't find anywhere else. While your work life tends to focus on economic concerns, professional growth, achieving personal success and satisfaction, volunteering focuses on the quality of life and wellbeing of other people and society as a whole. Volunteerism fosters values of compassion, cooperation, solidarity, reciprocity, mutual trust, belonging and empowerment. These are things that make the world a better place for everyone.

Volunteering is a beautiful gift for you and your community. If you are feeling unsure about what to do with your life, or if you feel you need direction, volunteering can offer some perspective. Volunteering is an excellent way to explore different interests or to investigate what you are passionate about.

Volunteerism has multiple benefits to one's wellbeing. It can help combat depression and counteract the effects of stress, anxiety, and anger. It can also improve one's self-confidence and self-esteem while providing a sense of purpose. Volunteer work is both meaningful and satisfying. Plus, it can be a healthy way to relax or re-invigorate your energy level. It's a wonderful way to mix up the day-to-day routine of work, school, or other commitments. And it can provide a renewed sense of creativity, motivation, and vision for your personal and professional life.

Instant gratification and sentiments like, "What can the world offer me?" are pervasive in our twenty-first-century world. Our ubiquitous connectivity to information and technology has placated us into believing that everyone has access to the same opportunities in life. Instead of standing around, waiting for the world to offer up its bounty, wouldn't it benefit us all if we individually offered our unique talents to the world? It's surprising what can happen when you give a little. The world is difficult enough as it is. Why not help each other out? I spend my Wednesday evenings teaching yoga at a free clinic as part of a healthy-living program. My dear friend Heidi spends time taking care of cat colonies throughout Salt Lake. My colleague Kennedy gives back to homeless youth and the LGTBQ community. My friend Charlie helps adopt, foster and care for dogs. Everyone has something to offer.

You may volunteer for an organization and feel like it's not a good fit. That's okay! It's like finding a good hairdresser; you may need to explore a few options until you land on the volunteer opportunity that is good for you and the organization.

Story Time!

I love cats! They are my favorite animals, and I have loved them since I was a small child. The first time I did volunteer work (at the age of 12) it was at my local animal shelter. I volunteered every Saturday, playing with the cats, brushing them, feeding them, and helping to get them adopted. At 12 years old, I wasn't the most helpful set of hands, but I enjoyed being around the cats and I learned a lot.

At 16 I volunteered at the Utah Pride Center in their Youth Activity Center. This led to a fulltime position two years later. I have also volunteered at Expos like the Outdoor Retailers and a variety of different local hair shows. Currently, I spend every Wednesday night at the Maliheh Free Clinic teaching yoga to their patients.

Over the last 18 years I have volunteered at countless organizations and each one had a reward. Not only did I get that warm fuzzy feeling for helping out, but I made life time friends, was presented job opportunities, and volunteering lead to other opportunities to explore myself and my interests.

Writing Exercise: What are Your Values?

Identifying and understanding your values can be challenging, yet it's a vital exercise to undertake if you want build and support healthy relationships. If you can articulate what's most important in life, you can find people and communities that understand and support you on your journey toward success. This writing exercise will help you define what you value most. Remember, values are things you believe are important to the way you live and work. They determine your priorities, and they are the measures you use to determine if your life is turning out the way you want it to. When your actions and behaviors match your values, life just feels good.

Let's begin by using your tools for awareness: Think, Say, Act.

Think: Find a time and place where you can sit and contemplate. Look back on your life so far. Identify a few instances where you felt really good and confident about the choices you made. Is there a pattern to these moments in your life? Do they have a common thread? Next, identify a few times where you weren't so proud of the choices you made or the way you acted. Is there an underlying reason why you felt ashamed of the way you behaved?

Say: Read through the list below and pick out words that could define your values. Don't over think this step. Just write down values that jump out at you. Make a goal to identify at least 10 things you value. Write them down in your journal randomly. After you feel you have a satisfactory list, begin prioritizing your list. You'll want to narrow your choices to the top three. A good strategy to make this easier is to visualize a situation where you might have to make a choice between different values. Which would you choose? Make sure each value fits with your life and your vision for yourself. Do they make you feel good about yourself? Are you proud of them? Would you feel comfortable and proud to share your values with people you respect and admire?

Accountability	Excellence	Perfection
Accuracy	Excitement	Piety

Achievement
Adventurous
Altruism
Ambition
Assertiveness
Balance
Being the best
Belonging
Boldness
Calmness
Carefulness
Challenge
Cheerfulness
Clear-
mindedness
Commitment
Community
Compassion
Competitive
Consistency
Contentment
Continuous
Improvement
Contribution
Control
Cooperation
Correctness
Courtesy
Creativity
Curiosity
Decisiveness
Democraticness

Expertise
Exploration
Expressive
Fairness
Faith
Family-
oriented
Fidelity
Fitness
Fluency
Focus
Freedom
Fun
Generosity
Goodness
Grace
Growth
Happiness
Hard Work
Health
Helping
Society
Holiness
Honesty
Honor
Humility
Independent
Ingenuity
Inner
Harmony
Inquisitive
Insightfulness

Positivity
Practicality
Preparedness
Professional
Prudence
Quality-
orientation
Reliability
Resourceful
Restraint
Results-
oriented
Rigor
Security
Self-
actualization
Self-control
Selflessness
Self-reliance
Sensitivity
Serenity
Service
Shrewdness
Simplicity
Soundness
Speed
Spontaneity
Stability
Strategic
Strength
Structure
Success

Dependability	Intelligence	Support
Determination	Intellectual	Teamwork
Devoutness	Status	Temperance
Diligence	Intuition	Thankfulness
Discipline	Joy	Thoroughness
Discretion	Justice	Thoughtfulness
Diversity	Leadership	Timeliness
Dynamism	Legacy	Tolerance
Economy	Love	Traditionalism
Effectiveness	Loyalty	Trustworthiness
Efficiency	Making a	Truth-seeking
Elegance	difference	Understanding
Empathy	Mastery	Uniqueness
Enjoyment	Merit	Unity
Enthusiasm	Obedience	Usefulness
Equality	Openness	Vision
	Order	Vitality
	Originality	
	Patriotism	

Act: After you have your top 3 values listed and written in your journal, it's time to make a commitment to uphold your values and to find people and communities that support or respect your values. You'll want to think about how this might apply to your personal life and work life. Take a moment to construct a commitment statement, maybe something like this:

I commit to making cooperation a value that I let drive my choices, actions, and beliefs.

I commit to seeking out people and communities that support my value of cooperation.

The final step to act upon is to seek out a new community or group that you think might help you incorporate your values into your everyday life. You can join a group that is already organized or you may want to start your own. Think about how starting a book club, a hiking group, or a coffee meet up with colleagues might open up new opportunities for connection.

RECAP:
Connecting with other people expands our worldview.

Look for communities, networks, or groups with a shared purpose and a broader perspective.

Volunteering is the best way to create connections and to find passions in life.

Find your values and get out there and immerse yourself in a community.

Chapter 8 Conclusion
Bringing it all together

"The end of a melody is not its goal: but nonetheless, had the melody not reached its end it would not have reached its goal either. A parable."
—Friedrich Nietzsche

By reading this book and doing the work, you have taken a giant leap forward in creating a life full of growth, success, and fulfillment. But the work does not end here. As you continue in your career and your path in life, there will always be ample opportunity to practice what you have learned here. You will experience moments when your patterns and boundaries are challenged. And there will be times when your values and priorities shift because you hit a new developmental stage. It is a process we all go through. Everything is in constant motion and flux. But if you continue the work you've begun, and recommit yourself daily to the development of patterns and a system of self-care that supports your growth, you can forge the life you desire.

There are days when I wake up not feeling my best. And sometimes all I can feel is fear. There are days I fall back into old patterns and break my boundaries. And there are times when I am less empathic towards other people because of my own self-imposed drama. In these moments, I try to remind myself that I still have options. I have a choice—I can be crippled by my feelings, or I can take steps to conquer them. We are human. We are remarkably imperfect. And this life holds many challenges. When life serves you a barrage of painful trials, stick to your guns.

Take one day at a time, and try your best. If you try your best, no matter how the day presents itself, you'll find success in this work and in your life.

Creating Social Change

All the ideas and work presented here were developed to assist you in creating the future you deserve. Creating healthy patterns, boundaries and a system of self-care will help you perform at your highest level and operate at your fullest potential. The information here is also designed to create a better community around you. The ideas expressed on community and empathy are explained in a manner to help you in your personal and professional life, but the concepts also facilitate social change on an individual level.

While I was working on this book, I read *Radical Dharma: Talking Race, Love, and Liberation* by Angel Kyodo Williams and Lama Rod Owens. This book is an unapologetic discussion about racial injustice. One quote in particular from the book hit me like a ton of bricks: "I don't have time for y'all's self-care bullshit. We are out here facing real shit! Keep that to yourself."

It's true, there are people and communities out there who are fighting real shit—racial injustice, religious intolerance, gender inequality, poverty, debt, disasters, the list goes on. But this does not negate the fact that true change begins with the individual; it begins with just one person. You can't change the world if you are a mess. With this work, you have an opportunity to use healthy patterns and genuine empathy to fight the injustices of the world. (This is one of many reasons why I encourage everyone to get out there and volunteer.) You have the capacity to help those who are in times of need and struggle. You can be a voice for those who don't have one. You can push for change by standing up for what you believe in.

Use the progress you have achieved here to not only to shift your own life, but also to shift the world around you. Once you have some equilibrium in your own life, revisit this work and approach it from the angle of, "How can I make the world a better place by developing healthy patterns?" Perhaps you'll start small by recycling more. Or you might make a decision to jump into local politics, or educate yourself on issues around race, class, and gender. Our patterns do make waves—they ripple across other people's lives and within our communities. Next time you revisit this work, see how you can create patterns that make the world a kinder and easier place for all of us to live.

Writing Exercise: Vision Board

I would like to give you one final exercise to bring together all the work accomplished. It's time to make a vision board based on what you've learned from your experiences with this book.

It's quite simple really. A vision board is a tool you can use to help clarify, codify or maintain focus on your goals. All you need is a poster board to which you will add words, pictures, poems, inspirational thoughts (the sky is the limit here), anything that is a visual reminder for the commitments you've made as you worked your way through this book. It is also a place to celebrate your wins. Make sure to add details that show your progress as well as things you want to continue working on.

Every January I make a new vision board based on the work I've accomplished from the previous year. I use it as a daily visual reminder to stay committed to creating healthy patterns, boundaries, self-care, empathy and connections. If you plan on expanding by volunteering or creating social change, include that on your vision board as well.

Spend as much time as you can on your vision board. Allow this board to be your constant reminder of the ways you will recommit yourself to the process of growth. Let this be your vision for the future. Let it reflect all the progress you want to achieve and all the goals you wish to accomplish. This will be a visual reminder of who you are and how you will continue to blossom in the world. If you feel you need help starting your board or would like some inspiration, Google *Vision Board*. There are countless videos and tutorials on how to create one.

Coming back to fear

I began this book by writing about fear, and I would like to address fear at the end of this process as well. Bringing your fears to the front, allowing yourself to be honest and vulnerable is a good thing. It's helpful to recognize and acknowledge your fears. Revisit your first journal entry regarding fear. Ask yourself, "Do these fears control me or do I control them?" Sure, some of your fears may always be with you—fear of death, disease, illness, etc.—but did you create new patterns that allow you to control your fears? Did you set up new boundaries that eliminated a fear or two? Did learning more about connection and empathy help dissolve or soften a fear?

My goal was to give you the tools to elevate your life. But I also wanted to show you that fear (even though it's a necessary part of life) doesn't have to be an insurmountable wall. You have the ability to mitigate the fear in your life. You don't have to let it control how you live. Don't let fear stop you from working on yourself, exploring opportunities, or taking risks. Remember, a life with no risk, is a life with no gain.

Journey on

Moving forward, remember to Think, Say, and Act. In my experience, these three simple actions are steppingstones toward accomplishing your goals, achieving growth, and maintaining a life you want and deserve. Remove any one of these three actions and the formula for success is incomplete.

As a final note, I want to congratulate you on taking a risk and putting in the work. There are so many wonderful experiences ahead of you. Journey on my friend! And may the skills and lessons taught here provide you with valuable tools with which to navigate success. If you ever doubt yourself or feel that you've lost track, come back to this text or revisit your writing exercises. Coming back to what you have learned and recommit yourself to the process of change. It will always be here.

There is no one like you. Celebrate the wonderful being that you are! I thank you for taking the time to join me on this journey.

Until next time,

Daniel Jacob Hill

Guided meditations

These guided meditations are here for you to use anytime and anywhere. They can assist you in maintaining a daily mediation practice or help you through moments of emotional distress. Meditation is a great tool to lean into when you are feeling intense emotions like anxiety, stress and fear. These exercises help ground you back into yourself and allow you to move about your day with more ease and flow.

Make a commitment to mediate daily for twenty minutes. If twenty minutes is challenging, begin with five minutes and work up to twenty. Find a comfortable, quiet spot to meditate in, and find a meditation posture that suits your body. You can try each of the guided meditations or just choose the ones that speak to you.

Here and Now

This is my favorite meditation. It is a practice that can be used every day for twenty minutes or as a quick grounding exercise to bring you back into the present.

Start in a comfortable seated position, close your eyes and begin to focus on your inhale and exhale. As you continue to breath, draw your attention inward and repeat the phrase, "I am here, and the time is now." With every inhale and every exhale, repeat this phrase.

This meditation is ideal for those moments when you are feeling stressed or overwhelmed. This practice brings you back into yourself and reminds you that you should be focusing on the present. Whatever stresses are happening in the world around you, you can find strength in the present moment. There is no reason to let your mind get muddled up by the story-telling ego. Let go of "should"—where you should be, what you should be doing, who you should be. Focus on what is good about here and now.

Counted breath

Start in a comfortable seated position. Close your eyes and begin to focus on your inhale and exhale. Don't change your natural breathing pattern, just observe it. After relaxing into the space, begin to lengthen the inhale and exhale, taking even breaths. Start by inhaling for five counts and exhaling for five counts. Then try six counts, slowly working your way up to ten counts. After doing three rounds of breath cycles of ten counts, begin to work backwards, doing a round of breath for nine counts, then eight, seven, all the way down to one.

This is a really fun meditation to play with. Try unique pattern variations; it's great way to focus your mind.

Candle Gazing

You will need a candle for this next practice. I recommend a non-scented candle. Scents may distract you from your practice.

Turn off all lights in your room, and light your candle. Assume a comfortable seated position. Taking nice, deep, even inhales and exhales as you begin to quiet your mind. As you breath, gaze at the flame of the candle. Gazing allows your mind to focus on the flame instead of distracting thoughts. This practice is good for relaxation and quieting an overactive mind.

Check in

Close your eyes or have a soft gaze on an object (this could be the floor, the wall, or incense). Allow yourself to quite your mind. If thoughts drift into your mind, acknowledging them and let them pass. Bring awareness to your breath, focusing on each inhale and each exhale. The breath has a soothing quality and will assist you finding focus.

 As you clear your mind of passing thoughts, turn your attention inward. Notice how your body is feeling. Check in with yourself. Scan your body, starting with your toes working all the way up to your head. Allow yourself to feel sensations you may be experiencing. If something is troubling you, meditate on that. Acknowledge it and acknowledge the sensations that your feelings induce. Perhaps you don't need to solve the problem. Maybe you can simply recognize the problem, feel the sensations it produces, and let it pass. Continue to filter through you thoughts as you focus on your breath and your body.

Appendix Resources

This resource list is designed to assist you and your client's needs. I have provided online resources and national resources to assist individuals with their needs. We aren't here to fix our clients, but we can guide them to people who can help. This is a resource list you will want readily available. As people in the service industry we encounter a variety of people with different needs. You will want to have this list handy in case you encounter an individual who needs some assistance. It's not your job to fix their problem, however you can assist them in seeking help.

Online Resources
Abuse
• Child Help Reporting child abuse
www.childhelp.org/hotline (800) 422.4453

• National Domestic Violence Hotline www.thehotline.org
(800) 799.7233

• National Sexual Assault Hotline rainn.org (800) 656-HOPE (4673)

• Drug Abuse National Helpline (800) 662-4357

• National Eating Disorders Association
www.nationaleatingdisorders.org (800) 931-2237

Immigration
• National Immigration Law Center www.nilc.org (213) 639-3900

• National Immigration Project of the National Lawyers Guild www.nationalimmigrationproject.org (617) 227-9727

LGBT+

• GLAAD: For over 30 years, has been at the forefront of cultural change, accelerating acceptance for the LGBTQ community. www.glaad.org/resourcelist

• The Trevor Project: Assistance for LGBTQ+ youth. www.thetrevorproject.org (866) 488-7386

• Trans Life National Hotline: Assistance to transgender people. www.translifeline.org (877) 565-8860

Mental Health

• National Suicide Prevention Hotline (800) 273.8255

• Psychology Today: Assistance in finding a psychologist. www.psychologytoday.com

• Volunteers of America: Help with individuals with mental disorders and homelessness. www.voa.org

Appendix References

Throughout this book I referenced to this Appendix where you can find a vast majority of tools to assist you in reaching your full potential. The best place to start is by visiting the website, www.mypatternbreaker.com there you will find resources from daily meditation practices to videos for a daily yoga practice at home. The site is an online resource center to assist you in your journey.

Recommended Reads

Broken up into categories I have provided some recommended reads that I found useful and perhaps they may be of help in your journey.

Cooking

Fast, Fresh & Vegetarian; *John Ettinger*

The Everyday Ayurveda Cookbook; *Kate O'Donnell*

Veganomicon; *Isa Chandra & Terry Hope Romero*

Mind Body Green Mindfulness, food, exercise, and more https://www.mindbodygreen.com/

Fitness

Classpass: Fitness and exercise https://classpass.com/

REI: Outdoor activities and events https://www.rei.com/events

Personal Growth/Self-Help

Conscious Living; *Gay Hendricks*

The Big Leap; Gay Hendricks

The Gifts of Imperfection; Berne Brown

The Four Agreements; Don Miguel Ruiz

Psychology
Race, Class, and Gender in the United States; *Paula S. Rothernberg*

A Geography of Time; *Robert Levine*

Dr Brené Brown: Empathy vs Sympathy; see Twenty-One Toys https://twentyonetoys.com/blogs/teaching-empathy/brene-brown-empathy-vs-sympathy

Dr Brene Brown; TED
https://www.ted.com/speakers/brene_brown

Gaur Gopal Das; Goalcast
https://www.youtube.com/watch?v=cyaFMYWA0Qk

Sobriety
The 30-Day Sobriety Solution; *Dave Andrews and Jack Canfield*

Dead Set on Living; *Chris Grosso with Alice Peck*

Spiritual
The Baghavad Gita; *Stephen Mitchell*

Way of the Peaceful Warrior; *Dan Millman*

Success and Motivation
Life as a Daymaker; *David Wagner*

Rhinoceros Success; *Scott Alexander*

Stealing Fire; *Steven Kotler & Jamie Wheal*

Yoga/Meditation
The Heart of Yoga; *T.K.V. Desikachar*

Age Less; *Sharath Jois*

Mind, Body & Spirit; *Donna Farhi*

Journey into Yin Yoga; *Travis Elliot*

Meditation exercises and inspiration for well-being; *Bill Anderton*